DELIRIUM DIARIES

"I raced through this emotional rollercoaster of a book with both horror and awesome admiration. Pete has written an utterly absorbing and emotional account of his ordeal. What really shines out from the page is a total lack of self-pity."

Michael Taylor
TheBusinessDesk.com

DELIRIUM

DIARIES

Pete Mackenzie Hodge

The Book Guild Ltd

First published in Great Britain in 2024 by
The Book Guild Ltd
Unit E2 Airfield Business Park,
Harrison Road, Market Harborough,
Leicestershire. LE16 7UL
Tel: 0116 2792299
www.bookguild.co.uk
Email: info@bookguild.co.uk
X: @bookguild

Typeset in 11pt Minion Pro

Printed on FSC accredited paper
Printed and bound in Great Britain by 4edge Limited

ISBN 978 1835740 729

British Library Cataloguing in Publication Data.
A catalogue record for this book is available from the British Library.

For Nikki, Hazel, my family, and friends

There's a quote from Bukowski, that I love:
                    "Once you've been to hell and back,
            you don't look behind you when the floor creaks
                    and the sun is always up at midnight
                        and things like the eyes of mice
                    or an abandoned tire in a vacant lot
                            can make you smile
                    once you've been to hell and back."

I've known Pete a while; I have his first prosthetic leg, which he gave me as a piece of art after losing the limb in a cancer operation as a young man. He sprayed it Jackson Pollock-style and gave it to me for my studio as a pot plant holder. When the more sophisticated robotic replacement arrived, he learned to walk again with it, and went all over the world.

I'm sure visiting the purgatorial dreamscape he describes here in *Delirium Diaries* qualifies as a particular type of hell.

The man is a walking miracle these days. Husband, father, touring musician (drummer!), transcendent author, and a glorious, spiritually charged ball of energy with an infectious personality.

Reading this gave me an appreciation of what we are capable of as a species when tested. And then, what happens when you beat the odds.

Read it yourself, you'll see.

You may even start to appreciate a few more of the small things.

Gavin Monaghan
Music producer and multi-instrumentalist, platinum &
gold sales credits, twice winner of BMA awards and owner of
Magic Garden Studio, England

PREFACE

We are in the twilight of winter lockdown; rules are easing. Released from containment and isolation, Nikki and I are out for our first meal since I fell ill. We are in the Lakes eating our meal outside in our coats and hats. Not allowed to be mixing indoors, in order to stop the spread. This meal feels well deserved after everything that has happened.

Midway through our dinner, underneath all the lights flickering, Nikki leans over and says to me, "Alan Partridge is over there."

"You what?" I hastily reply.

"No, seriously, Coogan is over there."

I am dubious but glance over to check Nik's claim, just in case!

Fuck, it's him, it's Steve Coogan, one of my heroes, somebody who has made me laugh more than most.

I head inside to use the bathroom. I can't quite wrap my head around it. I return to our table; Nik gives me a mischievous smile. There is a momentary silence until I feel a presence to my right. I look over and nearly spit my drink everywhere!

It's him!

Mr Steve Coogan.

A national treasure.

"I believe you've not been very well, mate," utters Steve.

"Alright, Steve?!" is all I could muster in that moment.

Suddenly, we are engaged in conversation, covering everything from coma delirium, to the recent tragic passing of Steve's nephew, the pandemic, music and his current writing… which brings me onto why I am here, writing this and introducing my book.

"You should write about your experience," encourages Steve. "Just sit down and type and see where it takes you."

"I will do," I confirm.

After our whirlwind twenty-minute conversation, we said our farewells. Steve returned to his table, settled his bill and off he went in his maroon Mazda MX5, gravel rattling and crumbling underneath his tyres.

Nikki and I were then left flabbergasted and for the remainder of the meal, only capable of one thing: beaming with joy and laughing hysterically over what had just taken place. It dawned on me; it started to sink in that whilst I was in the bathroom, Nikki had courageously gone over to speak to Steve and explained what had recently happened to me and made sure to mention that I was a big fan of his work.

What an amazing thing to do for somebody.

Just as we prepared to head off ourselves, *things got brilliantly weird again…*

The waiter approached our table announcing… "I wanted to inform you that Mr Coogan has already settled your bill."

Nik and I didn't have any words left in us. We were on our way back to our Airbnb feeling very lucky, a feeling much missed indeed. Phone calls were made; I had to tell everyone I knew.

I couldn't believe it. You could almost feel the magic.

I will write about my experience.

I will write to heal myself.

I will write in the hope that others might relate to it.

And so I did…

CHAPTER ONE

To begin each chapter, a song has been chosen to best capture the emotion and story of the ordeal that I, family and friends faced as I fought for my life. Music is the core of my being, my escape, my companion as I journey through life. Music is the best healer and a friend for every mood and situation. Music is the very heartbeat of my soul and without it, I would not be here.

Tinseltown In the Rain by The Blue Nile

Tinseltown in the Rain *perfectly describes being locked down during Covid-19 in the UK: all of us dreaming of a better time, whilst doing the best we could with the cards we were dealt. This song to me is about longing, love, and false hopes and promises.*

Have you ever had a nightmare that forces you to awake in sheer terror, which then leads to a deep fear of falling back asleep? The ones that leave you almost paralysed, paranoid that you will keep ending up *again and again* in the endless cycle of traumatic dreams? The ones that no matter how exhausted you are, or how much you really need the sleep, the last thing you want is to go back to that place. The truth is that we have all felt this from time to time, and if we're honest, we probably dread the next time one comes along and interrupts us sleeping. Now I want you to imagine this reoccurring again and again, a nightmare re-emerging, resurfacing, over and over without a pause. Each time getting more and more bizarre, yet all still very real and vivid. Trapped in the noxious realm of broken dreams. A dimension of fear. Imprisoned by its terror. A space so bad that it's impossible to even imagine escaping from its cruel grasp. There is no escape. You are completely alone, forever, save for a miracle. A stroke of immense luck. A one in a million kind of situation.

What the fuck is happening? It is Christmastime, 2020. 2020 will be remembered as a year of soaring highs and crippling lows. From the bleary-eyed peak: the joyful, serene bliss of the birth of our precious baby daughter, Hazel, who was born in February (following four rounds of IVF), to the other end of the scale: being locked away from everyone and everything, in isolation due to the Covid-19 pandemic that effectively made the world fall apart with still no real sign of things improving anytime soon. Right now, this winter could spell further disaster for our health system, the frontline staff and everybody's search for their lost freedom.

This festive season feels much like any other Christmastime. The weather is bleak, cold and wintery – but not in a dreamy, white and fluffy Christmas card kind of way. Didn't we used to have those when we were younger? It never really seems to snow at Christmastime anymore, does it? If it does, it is the kind that feels like bird shit slush slapping down on the back of your neck before descending to the ground and turning into a polluted, grey mush – a perfect bath for the diseased rats. The clouds hang low this season, making us feel more claustrophobic than ever. Icy rain has been pouring down for days and it doesn't seem to be letting up anytime soon.

I agree to meet up with my friend Martin Brick outdoors, as it is illegal to meet up with people indoors due to lockdown rules. This year, we organise our annual festive catch-up to take place on the streets of Kings Heath, *out in the elements*, in a bid to stop the spread of the virus and avoid a hefty fine. Having not seen anyone outside of my bubble for what seems like an eternity, I am keen to have a laugh and blow away those lockdown cobwebs in an attempt to muster up some much-starved festive cheer! Armed with a Tommee Tippee baby milk flask containing healthy measures of Jameson, coffee and plenty of sugar (it is the festive season after all!), I hoist myself into my Uber, the interior of which possesses a clinical clear PVC barrier separating me from my masked driver. I feel claustrophobic.

My destination today is Kings Heath High Street, South Birmingham, as we are down visiting the in-laws. Now, the only reservation I have about my impending outdoor knees-up is the fact that, in all honesty, I feel pretty run down and have done for quite a few weeks. In my eyes, I'm not run down enough to be *in bed* but feeling, as Withnail puts so succinctly, 'Like a pig has shat in my head.' I think I feel off colour recently because I have been isolating at home for the past couple of weeks, having come into contact with two work colleagues who have tested positive with Covid-19. Despite having had numerous tests showing a negative test result, I have been feeling under the weather since mid-December onwards, and were I more sensible, I would take this as a message from my body to rest up, in order to be fighting fit for the forthcoming festive frolics. To be honest, I feel like I will never feel *well* again, not in the real sense at least. It feels *that long* since my body has felt at full health. Despite all this, my stubbornness is activated. I won't be told. My FOMO has well and truly kicked in.

I was due to meet Martin at 3pm in the driving, 0.5 degree rain outdoors. My thoughts are basically that Covid would not stop me; it's already robbed us of the things we loved for far too long now. Life without gigs, football, theatre, meals out, festivals… I could go on! Bleak times indeed.

I arrive slightly early. It's 3pm and it's *already dark*. I take up my position beneath the dilapidated, now obsolete cinema under a dimly lit shelter. The plan is to go to the outdoor festive market but for now, the order of the day is to try and keep warm whilst taking in this year's somewhat eerie and subdued pre-Christmas rush. The high street shops and cafes are closed save for a few pound shops, takeaways, and pet shops (we'll come to that later!). The traffic is thick, with cars and buses packed in tightly, creeping slowly to who knows where. Perhaps they are sat in their cars, crawling along, just to get out of the house for a while and beat the lockdown boredom? My subconscious is aware of the exhaust fumes of engine traffic rising up against the harsh, freezing rain and hitting the ceiling of a thick blanket of cloud. The feeling of lockdown entrapment is even more intensified by this smog.

This afternoon, the clouds are encasing our world, trapping any chance of seeing stars, fireworks or the moon. You can forget the stereotypical hallmark sights of starry nights, sleighs, and reindeer. The pandemic has other ideas, more sinister ones. I feel that *this* Christmas, we are going to need to *try* extra hard to have fun with limited energies, patience and hope in the air after the year of extreme compromise, tested patience and sacrifice which has become the *new normal*, as they say. Today, the street feels totally polluted with the worst kind of fumes circling past each needled necklace of rain. Like the last of the earth's oxygen has been gobbled up by an invisible monster, replaced with an unwanted gift for our lungs: smog. This smog forces our bodies to adjust to feeding off the gusts of spluttering exhaust waste and rely on our respiratory capabilities. Lack of air quality is not at the forefront of my mind; however, it is screamingly noticeable at the back of my initial thoughts, which are focused on gaining relief from the months of shacked up boredom by enjoying a rare chance to socialise. The only thing on my mind today is to have fun with an old friend and laugh at our seemingly stupid idea of having a two-man Christmas party outside in the rain. We're all dressed up with nowhere to go.

Martin arrives clutching his own flask containing whiskey and caffeine, and after our initial greeting using the now toe-curlingly cringe method of bumping elbows (Covid measures again), we proceed in pouring ourselves a drink from our respective vessels. As I grab my baby flask out of my wife's bum bag (classy), I take a guess at how to operate the thing. There is what seems like a simple open/close button function on the baffling container, yet having pressed the button, I tilt the flask to check if it is now pourable and in doing so, I accidentally pour scolding hot Irish coffee all over my hand! As I look at Martin, he can only stare in bewilderment with a look that screams *things can only get better*. Not a good start; possibly an omen of things to come. Having boiled part of my hand with the wasted whiskey, we eventually enjoy a mug of our festive punch, which temporarily warms us, albeit it is only short-lived due to the decreasing temperature.

Like whenever we meet up, Martin and I chat about all things comical and politically grave, our respective football teams, and, of course, music. Martin then suddenly realises that he has lost his face mask en route to meet me because, *yes*, it's 2020 and it is now *the norm* to leave the house with a blue, almost dental-looking surgical mask made of polyester, our special kind of a *face nappy*. How things have changed in the space of a few months! Nowadays, if anyone is seen weaving across a shop floor, or let's say, ambling down the bog roll aisle in a supermarket *without* said mask, they are seen as ignorant, probably a Covid denier who has zero concern for you or anyone else's health and safety whilst they're without a doubt stockpiling a year's collection of shit tickets, leaving insufficient supply for everyone else.

Tracing back Martin's steps to look for his mask, we walk briskly against the howling weather and the crawling traffic up Kings Heath High Street, past the sorry sight of the *closed pubs*. It's a sad, sorry sight to see the legendary music venue Hare & Hounds all locked up and lifeless – a far cry from its usual hustle and bustle. Closed pubs, *at freaking Christmastime*. Martin stops every few steps attempting to ignite his cigarette lighter, his hand cupped over the translucent, battery-sized blue gas container. In the end, we elect to head back to his house for a replacement face mask as he has no luck in finding his original one. Once he finds a substitute face veil, we're heading back on the opposite side of the high street, where the only shops that are open are the likes of Poundstretcher, Greggs, and off-licenses – all deemed *essential* in the government's eyes. I cannot remember whose idea it was to go to our next location, but either way, it serves to keep us from arriving at our early deaths. (More on that bombshell later!)

Like a pair of washed-up vagrants, we enter the local pet shop and laugh uncontrollably at the grotesque, vile sight and stench of dog treats – dried up pig's ears, cow trachea chews, pig snouts, knuckle bones, tripe sticks… I could go on, but I fear that nausea or much worse could ensue! We head deeper into the shop and even though I am still wearing a mask, I feel endangered. More specifically, I can feel in my very bones the danger of catching more virus and disease. We observe the seemingly cosy gerbils, hamsters, and rabbits, all unaware of the chaos occuring in the outside world, locked within sawdust, straw-bedded safety cells complete with running wheels and water bottles that have penne pasta-shaped metal nozzle ends stopping the rodents from gnawing their way out of *their very own* boredom and monotony.

Despite this humble setting, we are treated to the exotic sight and sounds of the in-house Macaw parrot whose name evades me (let's call him Colin for now). Colin the Macaw parrot, with his stunning turquoise and canary-yellow feathers, is an old, wise boy, the shop's shrewd observer for years. Martin and I stand, teeth still chattering from the cold, talking to Colin in voices one would adopt whilst speaking to a toddler. We're fully grown men! Colin is less than impressed and lets out a pitying squawk; our cue to scarper and complete our rendezvous towards the local Christmas market, which, today, is sparsely attended, giving off a muted, almost sombre vibe to the atmosphere. It seems all but some are at home, away from all of this.

We pass through the boutique stalls selling everything from jewellery and scented candles to other hippy goods and end up at the vinyl record stall. At this point, I know that I am *properly* ill as I simply can't even muster up the energy to sift through the racks of records. Instead, I stand stationary, staring at the bar and its light scattering of punters, thinking that booze is the last thing I want right now, while at the same time, my rain sodden beanie drips grey, smoky water onto my nose. Somehow my parka jacket (warmest coat I own) can't keep the cold out today. Its faux fur hood collects what feels like a mug's worth of chilly, dirty rain, which is now miserably drenching the skin around the back of my neck. It is time to go. Now. Order taxi, get indoors quick. Warm bath perhaps? Anything to thaw out this pitiful Covid-stained Christmas on the eve of Christmas eve.

I practically collapse into the back seat of Amar's Uber bound for my sister-in-law Gemma's house where my wife, Nikki, is sitting deservedly warm and snug. This taxi again is kitted out with a transparent plastic barrier which separates me from the driver, giving off the sense that the end of the world is somehow nigh. Amar is an eager talker. So am I, *usually*, but not right now. Not today, pal; not our day. Not one to take any convo-ending cues, Amar babbles on about the state of play with the pandemic, the lack of Christmas parties and how work is much quieter in town this year.

Upon arrival, Gemma and Nikki look at me as if I'm some sort of bum hailing from 'Gutterville'. I accept a bottle of cold Stella, but in all honesty, I should probably ask for a hot honey and lemon at this point. A few minutes later, I grumble the words, "I feel cold to the bone." And I do. I announce that, "I need a bath," to which Nik and Gem both agree, instantaneously. In a desperate attempt to thaw out, I begin to run a deep, hot bath and glug plenty of bubble bath into the now steamy tub. Anything to muster up some sort of luxury and comfort.

Once in the bath, it feels like respite from my recent endurance test. I feel almost tipsy with relief, mixed with a shadow of nausea. The next thing I feel is an unwelcome guest approaching my bodily system – one we are all familiar with – *the strike of a fever*. You just know when a fever is just around the corner, don't you? Like a freight train getting ready to flatten you. Cold Covid Christmas reality.

Once I get myself dressed and dried, I find myself downstairs again trying to discretely conceal my ailment in a bid to avoid being a party pooper against those trying to have an actual good end to their year. At this point, I know that a bed is the only place I should be – drugged up on over-the-counter meds or suchlike.

Fast forward to the next day at my in-laws, I try to put on a brave face for as long as possible whilst we watch some mushy American Christmas film, but I am barely able to hang on and I end up uncharacteristically announcing my retirement to bed. My hope is that I will feel better tomorrow for Christmas Day, where the plan is to celebrate with the in-laws at Gemma's. Now in bed in Nikki's parents' spare room, I feel like I am deteriorating rapidly, and, in my mind, I curse myself for being so gung-ho and adamantly stubborn in my insistence in meeting Martin yesterday. I notice I am coughing up phlegm and my temperature seems to be rising; the pools of sweat I now lie in are proof enough. What is it about Christmastime and illnesses?

Merry Christmas everyone, the 25th of December arrives, and a delicious full English brekkie is waiting for us downstairs, all laid out and ready on the dining room table. Still eager to power on, I put on a brave face and muster up what little energy that I have left to engage in conversation, and timidly pick at my cooked breakfast – not like me at all, as a fry-up is one of my favourite dishes to devour! Right now, I cannot help but notice how hot the room is, presumably from the cooking stoves; with winter central heating cranked up high and my fiendish fever spiking evidently by the minute, my case does not get much better! Alarmingly, I notice that each time I speak, my mouth becomes drier and drier, thus giving off the overwhelming sense of desperate thirst. Drier than the Gobi. I am worried. This now makes me fear that my 'winter lurgy' is something more threatening – something more vicious and rapid.

Breakfast complete, I dizzily stagger up the stairs of my in-laws' house and meet Nikki on the landing. There is something gravely wrong, and the uncertainty of what my ailment could be brings me to tears. I can't stop crying and I don't know why. Is it the worry of the possibility of an undiagnosed illness? Did I know what was to come? I follow my instinct, which tells me something *serious* is happening within me. This feels urgent. Act now, act now. I am desperate to be well again. I am beginning to struggle to breathe and need professional medical help *quickly*. Nik and I embrace and talk through what my next steps should be in the pursuit of unearthing what exactly is causing me to be so ill. Firstly, we agree that it is best for me to rest in bed again and not attend Gemma's get-together (something I feel very guilty about as I am fully aware of how much loving time and effort she has spent hosting today's gathering). Fearing it might be Covid, Nik and I decide that it is wise for me to book *yet another* C-19 test at the local drive-through testing centre. Evidence of my recent tests can be found in the passenger footwell in my car, with piles of polythene bags, nasal swabs that resemble ear buds, and cards containing QR codes. Mini mole hills of medical plastic debris; something you may find in a futuristic zombie, alien, nuclear apocalypse!

So here I am, driving to the test centre on Christmas of all days, with the hope that the flu capsules will now start kicking in and decrease my temperature. I feel more and more claustrophobic as the hours pass by and the already spinning walls feel like they may collapse on top of me as I reflect on how I've lost count of the number of tests I've had since September. I gag and cough as the swab tickles the back of my desert-dry throat as I circulate the plastic straw. I await the results to come back (usually within twenty-four hours if lucky) and I head back to my in-laws' spare bedroom, praying that I can find some rest in the midst of this chaos. I insist that I am OK alone in the house and that Nikki and Hazel join the rest of the family in their festive celebrations.

As the day progresses, I nestle under the duvet for hours on end, and due to shivering from the fever, I develop nasty phantom pains in my residual limb. These intermittent pains are becoming increasingly horrible to put up with, and they appear to be moving at a rather fast speed. Bolts of electrical stabbing pains add to my existing, awful symptoms (fever, dry mouth, hacking up green phlegm, trembling and sweating).

Not a good day. Or at least, not exactly how the 25th of December should be spent. Determined to get better, my intention is to rest up and drink plenty of water, a rather hopeful attempt in my quest to salvage some sort of Christmas.

Obviously bored, I take it upon myself to send photos of the aforementioned phlegm that I was coughing up into tissues to my family and friends, repulsing them with photos of the yellow matter that I was hacking up onto tissues. Alarming them, and probably having brought a little disgust upon their appetite for a Christmas meal at a nicely decorated table, they all seem a bit too eager for me to visit the walk-in centre. Our common goal is for me to get some antibiotics for what we all suspected to be a chest infection.

I arrive at the NHS walk-in centre, and after ringing the intercom buzzer, I provide them with Nikki's parents' address as we are down in Birmingham, visiting family (this is technically allowed as we are in a 'care bubble', as they like to call it).

The waiting room is closed to help prevent the spread of infection, so I patiently wait in my car for the GP to call me on my phone. Apparently, getting myself wrapped up resembling Sanka from *Cool Runnings* does not protect me from the cold, and so I turn my engine on and crank the heating up. It's taking *ages* for the doctor to ring, and it is tough luck that my patience today is wearing thin. I suddenly feel a fraction of movement and, turning my head, I notice a group of teenage lads, all dressed in black tracksuits. They appear to be picking up large pieces of abandoned glass and begin launching it onto a brick wall. The glass smashes into tiny pieces whilst the group laugh manically in unison.

Eventually the doctor calls, and she wastes no time as she informs me that she'll prescribe me with antibiotics and a nerve pain drug (amitriptyline) to help with the phantom pains. She trots out onto the car park, clip-clopping her high heels against the tarmac; the sound they produce makes my already throbbing headache feel unbearable. She hugs herself as she walks against the chill. No coat. She looks like an aging Bond girl from the '70s, full of faded glamour as if on her way to a fancy dinner party. I can't help but notice her surname on the prescription paper she gives me: *Dr Gotobed*. Go-to-bed. *What the actual fuck?* (I even clock that she has said name emblazoned across her convertible sports car in the form of a personalised registration plate!)

Once I am safely armed with my meds, I drive back to Nik's parents' house as I await the antibiotics to kick in and stop the grotesque catarrh that I keep ripping up every time I cough. As evening draws in, I am aware that I haven't eaten for a good while and upon Anthony's (Nik's brother) recommendation, I end up ordering a pizza from Domino's, secretly hoping that his claim on the thin crispy base being *the one* might be true. I eventually only manage to eat a single slice or two, leaving the rest in its box at the edge of the bed. *And so I stare at the red and blue pizza box on the floor whilst deeply hoping for an upturn in my condition, but cannot help sense a pull towards rock bottom.*

The next day, Nik and I arrive at the decision that it's best if we head back up north, both to protect others from my lurgy and for me to be able to seek urgent medical services. Nik does the driving whilst I sit beside our baby daughter, Hazel, in the back, donning my blue surgical mask for extra caution.

The journey begins and it's just about manageable until the sudden moment I notice a horrible taste and smell sensation resembling traffic fumes or cigarette smoke every time I breathe in. It feels as if I'm inhaling air from a car exhaust. Why on earth does it feel as if I can taste smoke? Is it pneumonia that I have after all?

We're about an hour away from home when I realise that I am becoming short of breath as we suddenly approach the most unwelcome of all traffic jams. I let out pitiful groans and start feeling very sorry for myself.

"I need my bed now… get me home, get me well," I hastily announce as Hazel glances in bewilderment at me, dummy in mouth, wide-eyed with those mesmerising puppy dog eyes. Even *she* looks concerned for my well-being. She's only a baby and yet she can somehow sense that something is up. I love her so much. I love Nik so much. My two lovely girls. I need to get well; I want to be well for them.

Another day, another spare room. I'm in a bed separate from Nikki not wanting her or Hazel to pick anything up from me. My condition is deteriorating as I notice that my urine has an alarming brown/orange colour. Do I have cancer again? It *better not* be cancer. I promise myself that I will not be tempted into googling my symptoms. I was already scared enough, certainly the last thing I needed was to read infinite possibilities of what my ailment could be. A doctor would be the one to diagnose me, wouldn't they?

My mum calls me having spoken to her GP friend up the road. The advice given is for me to drink eight pints of water *within the next hour* to flush out my system or my liver. I proceed to do as told! One thing I want to make clear is that drinking that much water in such a short space of time is harder than you might think. Perhaps most challenging of all is that I am struggling to catch my own breath when drinking, and so it is extremely disappointing how, after several pints, my urine remains the same dirty, stagnant brown colour. The amount of time I go on to spend waiting is too suspicious for my already troubled mind… Hours go by again with me in bed and with Nikki knowing there is something wrong. I am deteriorating rapidly and feel worse than ever before. It feels like the walls are closing in. Struggling to get oxygen.

Don't panic. Be with it all. Shall I meditate? Call 111? No, I think it's best we call for an ambulance. They'll take me straight to A&E and I'll be back in no time, right? Back for NYE at the latest, I reckon, no problem.

I am losing consciousness. I am dying. I think. We're all dying though, aren't we? I need medical attention and *quick*. Having called 999, the paramedics are taking an eternity to get here. Not their fault. They're understaffed and overstretched, at the busiest time of any normal year, let alone a pandemic winter.

I need an ambulance to arrive now.

I am in and out of consciousness.

I cannot really breathe.

Nik is ringing the 999 switchboard again; this is the third time.

"He is losing consciousness!" I hear her desperately say.

Finally…

Ambulance arrives

blue lights whipping in circular motions

illuminating the street with grave, clinical concern.

Neighbourhood drama

curtains twitch

I'd look too

wouldn't you?

Break the monotony of the year.

Hazel, my little girl, is asleep.

Doesn't know what is happening to her daddy.

How is she not waking up to sound of sirens?

I want to hold and kiss her.

I want Nik there too.

All of us together, embracing each other.

Safe from the world.

Our little family.

Paramedics hoist me onto a chair.

I have my prosthetic leg off.

Will I not need that?

I am wearing one trainer, a pair of Adidas trackie bottoms, and my dressing gown. Had it since I was twelve. Still has my name badge stitched on it. That name badge is the only thing providing me with just a fraction of sanity, the only reminder of how far I've come and how inappropriate it would be to give up the battle now.

Paramedics carefully lift me down the stairs of our house, scratching the paint on the wall in the process. If I don't make it, at least the marks will be a reminder of when I was last in the house. I feel like I'm a member of a sordid carnival, on my chair, my float being carried by the paramedics in some sort of depraved procession.

I'm outside in the cold night now, chair is at the bottom of a ramp that will help the paramedics move me into the brightly lit, sterile ambulance. Despite the chill in the air, I can feel the eyes of neighbourhood residents copping a glance at this yuletide drama unfolding before their eyes on our sleepy Mancunian suburban street.

Ah yes, the back of an ambulance. I remember this. I've been in one of these before. The young female paramedic (let's call her Tilly) gives me a jug of oxygen to chew on whilst she asks me questions about my life, family. Even cracks a few jokes. Pleasantries to keep patient from panicking. Tilly warns me that they may need to use the siren and not to be concerned if they do. I'm ready for whatever. Just get me to a place where I can be fixed and returned intact to my girls. To my life of abundant joy; my life of music, football, friendship and family. Back to my own little paradise. The siren kicks in but is underwhelming. I'm confused as to how quiet the siren screams are from within my neon box. Nothing like the deafening shrill you hear when one goes off outside. How ironic: the one actually inside the vehicle gets to see its quieter, somewhat calmer side while the outsider is given the angry waves of turbulent noise. I think Tilly is now holding my hand. Something that makes me want to cry; her concern for my well-being seems to be the tipping point that will make the iceberg of my manly front fall, allowing me to delve into the realm of my emotional side. I love her and I've only just met her; I love the guy who's driving us too – heroes on wheels dressed in green.

We are bound for Wythenshawe A&E, not Manchester Royal Infirmary as I had first assumed. I feel a lump at the back of my throat, and I fight back the tears. I wish this was Nikki's hand. I wish this was Hazel's hand. You are an angel though, Tilly – lady in green.

She intermittently checks my obs on her medical screen or device. She does well to hide her concern at my evident decline, I have to give that to her. How is Nik feeling now? What is she thinking? What is she doing? Thank God Hazel is too young to remember her daddy not being well. *Cannot die. Must not die.* What would be the point in that now? Is this really my time? Passing away, passing on from this life away from my girls is simply not an option. *It can't be an option.* We will fight this. We will fight this. What a waste it would be to not be around to witness my girl growing up. What a crying shame that would that be. To not *be there* for her school assembly performances, help her learn to ride a bike, watch her blow out the candles on her birthday cake, wipe away her tears on her wedding day, take a picture of her on graduation day. If there's anything to fight for, it's Hazel. If there's anything to fight for, it's Nikki. They are the wind leading me in the right direction, and the footpath taking me back to where I belong.

CHAPTER TWO

If I Should Fall from Grace with God by The Pogues

In this chapter I describe the feeling that I am rapidly losing the battle to survive. I hear this song as a meditation on the trials and tribulations that we all must face up to in life. It is a song about hope, love and salvation that I hold on to.

Now I am in A&E at Wythenshawe Hospital. The haunting irony of being in the same hospital as the one Nikki gave birth in last year is not lost on me. That day of pure joy and relief!

Right now, in A and E my brain is *foggy*

I feel faint and weak, and my memory is fading

it is fading fast

it feels like my brain is shutting down, just like a half-fixed or half-broken computer

my organs are failing me, my own system turning its back on me after all we've been through

my body is switching off bit by bit

my hopes crumbling little by little

my eyes are red raw and they sting

the lights of the hospital not helping, not helping at all

my sinuses are in agony

I cannot really breathe

cannot really speak

I try to explain the timeline of events that got me into this predicament to the medics

I struggle to get my words out

I feel breathless whilst spelling out possible causes that could explain why I am so gravely ill

I believe I am waiting for a bed

I think I am in some sort of holding bay or corridor

am I lying on a stretcher?

It's busy here, busier than ever

feels like the hospital is bursting at the seams

I feel lonely and terrified

I'm not allowed to be scared though

this will hinder my forthcoming fight to survive

the one that would inevitably leave me unarmed

if the body and mind are calm, I *might* have a chance

it's the 27th of December 2020

peak of the second wave of the pandemic

couldn't have chosen a worse time to be admitted into the hospital

the staff are overrun, beyond exhausted

fragile sets of eyes everywhere, mine included

I look at a selfie I took before my journey in the ambulance, and, true to my suspicion, I look awful

eyes red raw, I am sweating

I have an almost yellow hue

I think I call Nikki when the signal allows me to

there is constant, loud beeping

the tests endless

bloods, temperature, oxygen levels, drips, heart rate…

I could go on
diagnose this one here
help him return home
we're all walking each other home
my mum receives a call from me
the same time her son receives a call to fight for his life
she hears a voice on the other end of the telephone
this is not her son
this is a frail, sick man fighting to stay alive
drowned out by the gushing of oxygen and crackling lungs
I can only muster between three and eight words, all of which circle my precarious mind
something along the lines of, "I'm going to ICU, they're putting me on ventilator."
I hang up. No energy left.

(In retrospect, thank God I didn't utter one of my doctors' written words to my mum: There are a few concerning red flags of something more sinister here… It was my mum I was talking to, after all. I didn't want to worry her more than she already would be upon hearing my frail voice.)

I sob into thin, polyester pillows
surrounded by plastic tubes and bleeping monitors
boiler-suited staff hurriedly go about their business in silence, hiding behind ghostly masks, white lies and empty words
if I can be certain of anything at this point, it is that they are suffering too.
That is for sure. Suffering for us all in here.
I could be wrong, but what I think happens next is that I agree to some sort of disclaimer

in case anything goes wrong and I cease to exist. You know, the usual.

I feebly agree to permit the medics to perform an intubation

an invasive procedure whereby they ram some tubes down my throat, down to my failing lungs for ventilating purposes.

This is all fine by me. I trust them. I say something along the lines of, "I have a wife and ten-month-old baby at home. I know you'll do your best for me."

Messages flood in, they keep coming and it's overwhelming. Hard to keep up. I can't actually read any of them, so the nurse does it for me. Even the inappropriate ones from Tom McG! I hate that this is happening. Loathe it. I hate the fact that I am making people worry. Right now, though, I feel loved. Love is all we truly need. It's the only thing capable of saving me now. I am no stranger to ICU, my new temporary accommodation for yet another time.

The messages keep flooding in, and I feel the love so much that I keep crying, my eyes ending up hurting more than ever. Someday, somehow, I'll be free from this awful suffering. There is the inevitable, all too familiar *why me?* train of thought. *What have I done to deserve this?*

At this point, I plummet hard and descend into a medical, drug-fuelled abyss.

My personal prison
fallen off a proverbial cliff
left my old life and my old self behind
long gone, my head is gone and I am elsewhere
I'm everywhere and nowhere at the same time
away from everyone and everything I love
I am no longer who I think I am

I have entered into dimensions unvisited before

I am lonelier than I have ever been in my entire life

feel like an isolated astronaut in space

more alone than a person caught in an avalanche

buried deep into the snow, I don't know which way to dig for air

there are people in blue suits and masks around me, surrounding me in the most suffocating way

I firmly believe that their intentions are not to be trusted

they have ulterior motives

I feel paranoid

I have signed my life away and there is no going back, no returning or taking it back

I am only a lab rat now

my only purpose is being the subject of a medical experiment

the subject lying decrepit in front of latex-gloved clipboards

do your worst, if you must

I accept whatever happens now

I *totally* surrender

I become one with it, aligning effortlessly with my fate

the most perfect, doomed and ill-fated constellation of stars

Upside down and torn apart

this will help my cause in the long run

don't fight it

don't let the bastards take you down

how am I to fight this?

I am weaker than a fly

my system the most hollow of all temples, the shallow water that almost kisses the brink messages from friends tell me to fight.

Making the first few particles of my shredded armour
suddenly rise

fight for my life.
This is a message to my body,
addressed to my constitution
fight and win at every cost
grit and determination.

From this moment onwards, I am completely unaware
of the order in which the following *dreams* occur. I don't
think chronology is important though. Perhaps the dreams
themselves are unimportant. What I do know, however, is
that they are real, real enough to leave a traumatic mark in
my spinning headspace. Some have plausible reasons for
cropping up. Linked perhaps to music I was listening to,
or places I have been or would like to visit. Other dreams I
believe occur for no rhyme or reason.

DREAM A

William, It Was Really Nothing by The Smiths

In this section of the book, I begin sharing the details I remember of my dream states. In Dream A, I am living through a gritty, unforgiving northern English scene. This song by The Smiths is a perfect portrayal of grim industrialism and grotesque mundanity.

I am in the 1970s, lying in a hospital bed in the North of England
I am on some sort of warped merry-go-round ride
clickity clack clickity clack
I smell coal and factory smoke
I can see nursing staff in dated uniform using archaic equipment, almost as outdated as this dream
I am well aware of the fact that I am a man from the year 2021
back in time
I am on an iron hospital bed
dozens of Florence Nightingales around me, forming the dome of my personal salvation

my hospital bed moves like a merry-go-round

a slow conveyer belt moving slowly, with its dominoes about to fall, standing tall right behind the edge

I see a chicken farm

I lie in my bed in a backless dress

maids and hens for company; somewhere in the turning wheels of my exhausted mind, the phrase 'misery loves company' smirks sardonically at me and my naked back

I can hear auld tyme gypsy fairground music

it's repetition is *maddening*

the rollercoaster slowly clatters along

I make out a workshop

almost Victorian in appearance

a man who is dressed like Fagin operates what looks like a steam railway

my own contemporary Fagin laughs with evil as he takes both my sanity and health

The Victorian 'receiver of goods' intruding in my era to take what's his

he is a large man with bushy, choppy sideburns

like Hilary Briss from *The League of Gentlemen*

he speaks to me in riddles and rhymes, casually messing with my mind

his accent reminds me of Tweedledee or Tweedledum from *Alice in Wonderland*

jolly and grating at the same time

he cackles a raspy, high-pitched self-conscious giggle after every ditty

I do not like his company; I want to be *far* away from here.

Momentarily, I cease moving altogether.

On the horizon, a poultry abattoir comes into view

feathers, blood and giblets

a creepy kitchen porter informs me that the hospital backs onto a farm.

DREAM B (PART ONE)

I Wanna Be Sedated by Ramones

At this point in my dream state, I am in dire need of being sedated or put to sleep due to the torturous tribulations I face during psychosis. I Wanna Be Sedated *evokes the simple yet aching desire to be put out of one's misery. The song reflects the desperate need to escape.*

I am in a high-rise office
sterile and clinical
hardback books spread out on the coffee table
a tall plant in the corner, probably fake
I am here for a medical trial
rewarded with a prosthesis with an ability to make me fly!
Sponsored by Adidas.
I pick up a book about retro football shirts.
  "*Thumb through the pages of that book, stop when you get to your team,*"
commands a Malaysian doctor in his late forties.
  I follow his instructions and come to a stop when I see a Blackburn shirt.

The doctor is called Ban Har

suddenly he shouts, "CHOP!"

The heavy book is forcefully slammed shut, my hand unable to escape its closing

I feel indescribable pain across my fingers

its burn shoots through every part of my body

I feel like I've been struck by lightning

I am in *agony.*

Ban Har and his sidekicks laugh hysterically, their mockery coming to them as easy as the air they breathe

I feel confused and humiliated

all I want is to go home

louder laughter, its echo seeming infinite

the air-con whirs its soulless air

water fountain humming in the background

I am cowering in the corner

I see a large boardroom table with steel legs, and in my troubled mind, it becomes the one where the looming decision whether to give me more life will be made.

Fire extinguisher, clinical, automatic lighting

I want to be in a jungle

I want to be in a desert Bedouin tent looking up at the starry sky

anywhere but here.

DREAM B (PART TWO)

Pyramid Song by Radiohead

Pyramid Song *is a meditative, enigmatic song with themes of life, death, and the afterlife. In the dream I describe below, I recall a space of losing control, deep fear of losing myself and the existential threat of dark forces. Slipping into the unknown.*

My hand is red raw
Ban Har mentions that he is an Arsenal supporter
apparently he hates my team, Blackburn Rovers
which must explain why he hurt my poor hand.
Fair enough
Ban Har tasks me to listen to snippets of music
my job for today is to try and guess the artist and song
names
I am in front of a white plastic screen
behind this screen is a festival tent filled with revellers
and ravers partying
like its 1999
they see me in a backless dress, humiliated and lonely
about to be the subject of a medical experiment

again, I am a rat inside the laboratory

the medics say I am *fortunate* to have been chosen to take part in it

they all act as if it is some kind of gift, a one-of-a-kind stroke of immense luck

I want no part in this whatsoever

none at all

I just want to go home! Is that too much to ask?

Each song snippet booms out of a PA system

every note being there to show me a snippet of how feeling alive can really be

how it is to hear your own blood sing in your veins

I know each and every track, off by heart

however, once when asked to recall them

my mind simply goes blank

someone has switched off my brain

the lights are on but no one's at home

they all mock as I quiver and rack my own brain

they play the music over and over again

without coming to a stop

but it is just no use

I am lost, I have become mute

I peer through the gap in the white screen

that separates me in sterile, medical hell

whose chemicals easily ignite its fuming flames

and those partying at the festival

they get to experience a different type of flame, the kind that so blissfully has you forgetting your own name

dancing, laughing, losing your inhibitions

I begin to realise I know some of these people

friends of friends

distant, yet familiar names

they call my name: "Hodgey! C'mon, Hodgey, you know these answers!"

They give me clues, really obvious clues
they too laugh mockingly and I am once again defeated
a fall from grace
I kind of want to die
what will my fate be now that I'm incapable of providing the right answers?

DREAM C (PART ONE)

Octopus's Garden by The Beatles

This song carries the clear, harmonious message of desire to be in a safe place, away from the threats and harm that engulf me, into a place of natural splendour. The dream I describe below finds me in a realm that I am desperately fighting to pull out of in the hope of escaping to safety.

I am on a hospital bed
surrounded by a medical mess
wires and tubes surrounding me
closing me in further into the white hospital walls
weaving out of my nose and mouth
the machines have taken over my body
and the medical demons of the 'what ifs' keep my mind captive
like ivy entangling an old garden shed
its dark green leaves hanging by a thread
this is dark and menacing
threats everywhere around me
do not trust their intentions

I have needles jabbed into my arms and wrist

I have invisible nails digging deep into my chest. I want my girls…

I am in a hazy, delirious state

the room first spins and then closes in on me

are there other patients here too?

Other experimentees?

A young, male doctor in his early thirties appears

he is dressed in what looks like a navy blue martial arts outfit

His garments are carefully ironed

he is well-groomed with healthy-looking skin.

I know this guy

I have met this guy before. A friend of a friend

Cuba is his name

"You alright, mate?"

"Ya'right, Hodgey lad?"

He calmly darts around the room from A to B

in a focused rush

he is clutching small electrical devices

with a clipboard in hand

I notice everything in the room has the Adidas logo on it

even my hospital gown, it too has the trefoil symbol on it, painted in black and white

I feel institutionalised; what an odd feeling

is this what I signed up for?

I have so many questions and they are all left answerless

I don't even know who I am anymore

I remember who I used to be and who I love

they are far, far away, in another realm, in another world

another dimension
will I ever see them again?
Will I ever be me again?

DREAM C (PART TWO)

Paranoid by Black Sabbath

This song strongly evokes the unease and deep-seated fear that I had towards the medical staff. I was convinced they were plotting against me, using me as the subject of some sort of sordid experiment. A paranoia I have never experience the likes of before.

The staff are on their busy mode, fully immersed in their
tasks
  they are preparing for some sort of launch or exhibition
  the room has a sterile, relaxed vibe to it
  I feel agitated
  severely paranoid
  I am locked to the bed with wires and tubes
  I have nowhere to go
  nowhere to run
  this is actual entrapment
  Cuba appears to notice my panic and despair
  he floats beside my bed clutching another foreign device
  almost as foreign as my own name today

again with wires and tubes dangling out of it

reminding me of its danger

this makes me even more fearful

before I get the chance to move away or put up resistance

he forcefully rams his palm onto my forehead

arching my neck back in the process

he pierces my nose with what looks like a clothes tag alarm

I quickly react and grab hold of his arms, trying to get him off me

fighting to get his powerful hands away from me

I try and fight him away from my personal space but it is *too late*

the shopping tag has somehow been attached onto my nose like a bullring

it seems that I am a magnet to pain

I am a moth to the flame

the doctors tell me to remain calm and to try and relax

relaxing here seems impossible

I am enraged and hopeless

my patience bursting at the seams

I yank at the clothes tag

it pulls my nose and turns it sore

I am branded cattle.

The jailer has thrown away the key

leaving me a helpless mess, and him a relentless, merciless man

I am surrounded by electrical tentacles

completely snared

nothing can help me now

I want to die.

I yell across to Cuba:

"What the *fuck* have you just put on me?"

"Don't worry about it, mate, just relax. We're only trying to help you."

"Are you for fucking real? Is this thing permanent?!"

"Don't fight it, mate. Don't resist, it'll just make it worse. Try and keep calm."

"Answer the fucking question. Is this thing permanent?!"

I yank violently and repeatedly at the tubes, with the device locked tightly to my nose

at least I can include it as one of my loyal companions in the midst of this chaos

the staff in their ridiculous blue kimonos hurriedly rush over for assistance

"Woah woah, stop that, Pete! Don't pull on it, you'll set the alarms off!"

I surrender

I am exhausted

I flop back onto the bed

I hate this place

I hate this bed

this is not my bed

not mine and Nikki's bed, with Hazel safely nestled between us

this is corporate, medical hell

the ugliest torment of it all

I am the subject of abuse, the essence of clinical experimentation

I am merely a cog in their machine

a patient number

no soul

nameless.

I am suspicious

my paranoia is heightening more and more by the minute

at last, I pretend to be asleep, albeit being more aware of conversations around me than ever before

I suddenly feel a presence to my left

I notice a man and a woman

both in Adidas kimonos whispering discretely to each other

the whole thing starting to feel like a conspiracy

the gown-wearing team are *up to something*

one is a young man, in his late twenties or so, with olive skin, dark eyes and bushy eyebrows

looks almost Arabic, Iranian perhaps

the girl looks Arabic too, also seemingly in her late twenties, tall, wearing a hijab

both have kind eyes, filled with a generous amount of compassion

I instantly warm to them

they are stood next to each other, their heads side by side

masks on, looking at a computer monitor screen

I get a sense that *they* are on my side

they seem to want to help my cause

I want to let them

I know they want me safely home, back to my own family

I know this to be true as I pick up on their hushed conversation

they do not want to be heard by Cuba or any of the senior staff

I pick up on the crux of their dialogue

they do not take kindly to what us patients are being put through

with furrowed brows, and worried brown eyes, they look

at the computer screen

both unaware that I am analysing their facial expressions and exchange of words

"*Have you seen this? What the fuck have they done to him? Look at those stats and the graph!*"

"*It isn't right. What are we gonna do?*"

"*We have to do something. Make it stop before it's too late for him. He has a young family, look.*"

They look up at my bedside counter, which has a framed photograph of me, Nikki and Hazel on top.

"*It's against basic human rights. We have to report this before it gets ugly.*"

They give me enormous comfort

free at last?

I have people on my side

they know I have been sold a lie and am in great danger

I feel a sense of *hope*

hope is the last one to die

one of my new friends says:

"*We'll think of a plan and make it right. Let's just sleep on it.*"

"*OK, my dear. Try and get some sleep.*

We have a couple of days off, so we'll head off but remember, stay strong and we love you."

And just like that…

they leave my bedside

they leave *my side*

my raised hopes begin to dissolve

a dark, brooding sense of fear and anguish sets into my psyche again

once again, my vision blurred, my eyes tightly closed

please don't leave me, friends

I go to sleep, though not forever, which deep down I want

I want to be asleep forever
so as to never wake up in this place again.

As my eyelids open, I notice Mr Ian Brown standing in front
of me
yes, that one!
Singer and frontman of The Stone Roses.
He too is dressed in a navy blue Adidas kimono
What might his business here be?
Is he part of their cult?
Is he in on it too?
Ian flits around the room along with the other staff
they are like bees in the busiest of hives
he checks devices alongside patients' bedsides
he winks at me before entering the manager's office
the office is next to my bed
an imposing room despite its small size
I feel like I'm in a ward in outer space.
No atmosphere.

I can't stop thinking about my two Arabic allies
the conversation that took place between them
I become excited at the thought of revealing it all
foul play occurring
Ian Brown is unaware this whole set up is detrimental to
us patients
did he honestly believe patients would be fitted with
groundbreaking prosthetic technology?
What if I told him the things overheard?
Would that help my cause at all?
I do not want my Arabic friends to get into trouble.

DREAM C (PART THREE)

A Day in a Life by The Beatles

*This song namechecks my hometown of Blackburn, which
I discuss in the dream state below, linking subjects of local
interest and other North West references such as local popular
culture and football. I chose this song as it fits perfectly into the
psychedelic, surrealist content of the dream.*

An air of expectation spreads across the ward
    strange, flashy exhibits of popular culture are being
erected beside patients' beds
    exhibits of famous bands – The Beatles, Rolling Stones,
Oasis, you name it
    even exhibits for both Manchester football clubs
    the kind you would find in modern museums
    replica giant guitars and drums
    yellow submarine hanging from the ceiling
    football boots in Perspex boxes
    fancy garments adorn professionally lit mannequins
    huge, colourful and enticing displays begin popping up
    kimono-donned staff pitch in to prepare for this
unknown event

the room transforms into a high-spec, fancy exhibition
who is it for? For what reason?
A DJ booth is set up
staff change records in between checking on medical devices
sounds of thumping, mechanical beats colliding with the medical beeping
house music blares out of this cavernous space
the lack of soft furnishings harshly ricochets the factoryesque rhythms
repetitive in nature to keep the staff in motion
evoking a sense of progression and purpose
Cuba and Ian shout down each other's ear lobes
they are agitated about something
paranoia in the air. Should be used to that by now...
out of nowhere, filing in one by one
the world's biggest names in music and sport trudge into the ward-cum-museum
they station themselves in front their respective exhibit
beside my bed are The Beatles
the fab four dressed as teddy boys
suited and booted, mop haircuts
John and George immortalised and reunited with Paul and Ringo
they plough through their old numbers
I am amused at Paul's innocence
his puppy dog eyes look longingly towards the corners of the room
shaggy hair flicking side to side.
How bizarre!
This is weird!
Stationed beside The Beatles are Oasis

brothers Liam and Noel Gallagher don their black shades

they mock the other bands, causing a stir

I am an onlooker to it all, but I am not invisible

I soak it in, let it consume me

lost in the intrigue of this moment, I forget my predicament

I witness as banter is lobbed back and forth between Oasis and The Beatles

and I welcome the distraction with open arms

jokes and digs made about each other's cities and football teams

strangely, I feel at ease with all this

Noel asks which football team I support, to which I reply with, "Blackburn Rovers."

His response is to laugh and say, "Fucking hell, we loved it when you beat the rags to the title in '95." The Beatles overhear this talk of Blackburn

John spiels off the story of the origins and meaning of their song *A Day in a Life*, which coincidently namechecks my hometown of Blackburn, putting me even more at ease

Wow, this is fucked up! Is that Madonna over there?!

I let each second ride into the next

I think the press have turned up as Noel and Liam begin signing rare Adidas trainers

they hand them to Cuba

he promises patients that we'll be gifted signed memorabilia upon discharge from 'the process', as he calls it

our mobile phones will also be returned to us seeing as they were 'confiscated' on our arrival

so that 'we didn't get too muddled'

or rather, that's the excuse they chose to use

I do not trust a single thing coming out of their mouths

the sight of our personal belongings
locked away in their mysterious office, making me even more suspicious
the rage inside me returns, building more intensely this time
it threatens to boil over
more relentless than ever
Ringo signs a bass drum skin for me
memorabilia of interest gifted to all of us patients
only to be locked away
just as out of reach as our personal state of health
it's my phone that I'm most bothered about –
my only contact back to life and any normality it used to carry
the world outside, thriving still
as vibrant and alive as ever
a sudden reminder of my predicament
my blood boils
all I want is my phone to call Nikki
to have her soothing voice brought back to me
for her to somehow organise a plan to come and get me
To get me the *hell out of here!*
I still have the tag on my nose FFS
stars of the rock 'n' roll world flood out after the initial buzz
John Squire turns to me as he leaves the room to my right,
"Thanks for that, Pete, that was ace," he utters as he exits.
Pep Guardiola leaves me with his Catalan smile as he files out of the room
the place is emptying quickly
the volume of the music decreases

slows the pace of the movement of the people in the room

it feels like the buzzkill at the end of a party when the house lights come up

the morning after a massive night

the calm after the storm

I am intent on fighting against the end of my old life as I knew it.

There is a sinister nature to the doctors

they waltz around, crack in-jokes, winking at each other

I am fed up and begin staring at Cuba and Ian with a glare that could kill.

Ian, it's a fix. The whole thing is a stitch up –

I know what they're up to

there is to be no benefit to us at all

they are trying to kill all of us innocent patients

stop them now, please, Ian, please!

I've got a young family and I need them, and I love them more than life itself!

Please help!

I plead and plead and *plead*

without shame

Ian responds with a raised brow, his face half a frown.

What d'ya mean, mate? I don't understand.

I begin to sing his song *Free My Way* whilst repeatedly pointing at the monitor screen to my left where my Arabic allies detected foul play. Singing Ian Brown's own song to the man himself, my voice shifts from a weak, subdued whisper to a loud, incensed crescendo as I belt out the passionate lyrics that grapple with heaven, the law, religion, and freedom.

(Cuba runs in panic, face blushing, sweat dripping down his brow.)

"What the *fuck* is going on?!"

Ian:

"There's a snake in the grass. C'mon, own up! Which one of you is it? Who's the grass!?"

(He looks around the room at each uniformed staff member, looking them straight in the eye, attempting to detect the guilty party or parties.)

I begin to lose it for what feels like the hundredth time tonight

I yank at the wires and tubes attached crudely to my nose

my movements fast and violent

Cuba is on the verge of a panic attack!

I laugh hysterically at my new-found power over these medical tyrants

I yank harder and, despite the pain, I repeat the harsh movement

I threaten to sound the alarms

the thought itself sends an adrenaline rush through my bones

I want to increase their panic!

I want to make some noise in this discreet hell, full of quiet, lying bastards

disturb their peace

it's their turn to suffer

Ian demands a private chat with Cuba in the office

trouble is, the office is walled with glass

myself and the other patients can see their interactions

we cannot hear it though

the vibe is negative and grave

their air suffocating

Ian and Cuba are now deep into an argument

my laughter is increasing with every pull I make at the tentacles wired to me with one hard, *colossal* tug, I finally rip out the tag!

Blood streams everywhere out of my nostrils, and all over the bed and floor in front of me

I *roar* with laughter!

I feel like a maniac, like King Lear

this is *their* predicament now, not mine

my previous desperation has spilled over

and I am now losing blood

more spilled blood!

More lost liquid!

I remind myself that *they* are now fucked, not me

alarms bleat out, sounding like deathly sirens

staff run towards my bed station, instruments always in hand

a doctor cries out for more assistance, which eventually comes.

A fluid as vile as war is slammed into one of my lines

leading its way into my veins

I am tranquilised.

In their eyes, I am an unwelcome rabid dog

they drug me back to where I belong

under their control, chained under their regime

the filth regain their power, my happy ever after drifting further away

a sleazy Cuba approaches with an ingenuine smile of concern.

I get the urge to snatch his mask off of his hideous face

"*You had us all worried there then, mate. That tag is to help you, trust me, pal.*"

He winks.

As soon as the words are said, I begin to sob

I sob all the pain out, letting it all escape me

I give in

I let go

a valley of tears and despair

a single moment of the ugliest of purges

I am ready to throw in the towel; I just want an end to this torment

right now, I want to die, become free at last

I tell the doctors in clear, lucid terms:

"I want no part in this anymore. I have reached the end. I redact my involvement and I want out. I want out *now!*"

"*But, mate, you're too far gone now. Too deep in, too tied. There's no going back. You've come so far; we cannot stop this in the middle of the process.*"

Cuba beckons Ian over as Ban Har stands behind the counter, looking all domineering and sinister.

"I'm done, Ian. I want out. I want no part in this anymore. I give up."

My head is in my hands

and I weep.

At this point, Cuba and Ian converse with each other, but keep their conversation to a whisper so that I cannot pick up what they are saying. This pisses me off even more; just when I couldn't feel any worse.

Conspiring prick number one finally speaks

Cuba: (coldly) "You've got two options. Either you carry on with this process or we turn off your machine."

Turn off my machine, I thought.

I know what this means.

This would be the end of me

every past memory and every future moment would be turned off too

my body would cease to exist

my heart would no longer feel

this machine was keeping me alive, just as I was keeping it running

granting it some sort of purpose, a futile goal

whilst they tested their new inventions out on me

on Nikki, on my little girl…

but it got too much

I simply had to die

the desperate hope of being reunited with my family had since gone

it was my time.

"*Turn it off then. Turn the fucking machine off. I don't care anymore. I want to die. Now,*" I announced, surrendering to the bleakness of infinity.

Ian responded:

"*C'mon, mate, you can't jack it all in now. You've got your whole life ahead of ya. Think of your poor family.*"

At this point it is too late

I arrive at my decision

I want to be alive no more

this is my time to go into the beyond

to the shore of elsewhere.

It was clear that Cuba had lost all of what little compassion he had left in him.

I was dead to him, insignificant

a piece of dirt on his shoe

everything sterile, soulless

this is not a place for me

I am not the subject of a medical experiment

I am somebody, a soul

a whole. A life.

Do not gamble on my life

I am powerless

I must leave this world behind

before anything else threatens to steal my dignity.

"Turn off the fucking machine… now!" I yell.

Cuba (angrily): *"Right, that's it, you've made your decision, perish in your basket, nice knowing ya, now fuck off!"*

At this moment, all fluids and signals cease pumping drugs into my body

the monitor screen to my left blinks off

my body begins to purge itself

I am shrinking

my soul journeys through my torso

it passes my neck and up, up, *up*!

through the crown of my head

I have exited the body

I feel peace

I feel oneness

I look down at my now shrunken, pitiful body

I was a visitor in my own guest house

I look down and notice my arms are stick thin

they have an almost jaundice, yellowy hue

below me, I notice a few stragglers from the exhibition

I make out George Harrison, who has noticed that they have turned off my machine

he realises I am in the midst of *passing away.*

"Someone stop this! Someone help, he's going, he's *on his way out!*" he cries.

Cuba: "It's too late, it's his own fault for ripping out his wires and tags, there's nothing else we can do for him."

I continue the process of *leaving my body*

I ascend up beyond the ceiling of the room

up, up, up and away
I am travelling on a kind of rollercoaster carriage
it ascends up metal tracks
I am moving at a snail's pace
I am inside a large, modern, glass building
I am dead as a doornail though
I have *died in hospital*
since gone
but still aware of the goings on in the streets outside
it is night-time.
I notice city lights and advertisements… LED projections.

DREAM D

Most of the Time by Bob Dylan

I remember that soon after waking up from the coma, I was in a very weak and emotional state, completely confused from the sheer delirium, feeling like my brain was totally jumbled up. I was utterly traumatised by the nightmares I experienced whilst in my coma. This song, produced by Daniel Lanois, really struck a chord with me as I navigated myself through the journey of healing, acceptance and endurance.

> I begin to see mine and Nikki's family members
> they are mourning the death of our daughter
> Again, I am in a fucking hospital bed witnessing this
> they clutch flowers and cards
> they are dressed in black and sobbing on the ward.

(This scene played out in my headspace after I woke from my coma and told nurses that Hazel was no longer with us. The nurses had to clarify this with Nikki over the telephone whether our daughter was, in fact, still alive!)

I notice my wife, Nikki,
she is in the bed opposite me
like me, she is gravely ill
neither of us able to muster up any strength to cry
similar to me, Nikki has a look of jaundice
she looks frail
like some sort of peasant
feeble, skeletal features.

DREAM E

Running Up That Hill (A Deal with God) by Kate Bush

More recently famous for its iconic inclusion in Stranger Things, *I relate closely to the song's themes of personal struggle and challenges, to my desperate need to escape my perceived reality and be back within the sacred sanctuary of my home, with my wife and daughter.*

I am shivering
I am in a desperate rush to escape Wythenshawe Hospital
I am in my hospital gown inundated with wires and tubes (alarms bleeping again!)
my arms are covered in blood
I have been pulling out wires and ripping off drips
I have somehow made my sorry way down to the ground floor in a giant service lift
I am somewhere at the back of the hospital
it is quiet around here, eerily so
I imagine this is the place where porters or kitchen staff ferry goods
or mortuary staff transport the dead

I am in a corridor and notice large, yellow toxic waste bins
garish warning signs emblazoned across them
the fire door is *open*
Could this be my escape route?!
I am pelted by a wintery, northerly gale
I look out of the fire exit door
I see the Manchester night
rain pelting down
street lights
post-festive, lockdown misery.
Porter:
"*What the hell are you doing down 'ere mate?*"
"I'm fucking leaving now. Right this minute. I need a
taxi home," I respond boldly.
"Whoa, hold on a minute! Look at state o'yer! Yer covered
in blood and wires, and you'll freeze going out like that."
I've been busted and snared
I weep again
no home time for me
I hear the echoing ring tones of walkie talkies
porter man calls for assistance to get me safely back to
the ward.

DREAM F

Helpless by Neil Young

Neil Young's Helpless *is a poignant song about the passage of time, memory, and the feelings of helplessness that often accompany life's inevitable challenges such as the one I and my family went through. It captures a deep longing for the comfort of the past, and in the dream I describe below, I am found at my wits end, desperate to turn back the hands of time.*

More *crisis.*

I am, once again, under the 'care' and control of Ban Har
he sits behind a miniature Zen garden,
strange-looking medical devices surrounding him
behind, what looks like a health and beauty spa is lit with neon coloured LEDs
I hear the fake sound of splashing water playing through cheap speakers
I notice a tank of small fish
(the kind of fish that eat the dead skin cells from people's feet)
I am agitated.

Ban Har speaks. "Pete, I am going to try something for you. You must listen to me and follow my instructions. I am going to take you into this room where the ladies will assist you."

I feel angry and helpless.

My bed is wheeled into the health spa.

I notice how dark the room is – like a nightclub,

the only lighting is the seedy neon pink illuminating the bubbles of water

this is anything but tranquil

the scantily-clad Asian women look drugged or brainwashed, or both.

I feel sad for them.

There is a sinister, sci-fi feel about this whole thing

if this was supposed to be a turn on, it was doing quite the opposite

I am terrified and repulsed

panicking again,

acutely aware that Ban Har has locked me inside this windowless, padded wet room.

I feel *trapped*

a million miles away from home

from Nikki and Hazel

wasn't I already dead?

I want to die *again*

this is hell.

Ban Har tries to reassure me. "All you have to do is breathe, Pete. Keep breathing and you will be rewarded."

I look up towards the ceiling and notice Cuba again

he is with a blonde woman

she's like a Barbie or a blow up doll

the creepiness intensifies

Cuba and his doll go in and out of automatic doors to luxury apartments
they look pleased with themselves
like they have won the lottery
gluttonous pride
Cuba notices me beneath him:
"Enjoying yourself, Hodgey lad? You keep that up and one of these apartments'll be yours, pal."
He winks.
I am struggling to breathe
feel as weak as a fly
water seems to rise up and I fear I will drown
I am in a chronic state of panic
fight or flight
I cannot move my body so I *punch*
my fists flail through the water
raining punches
but it's no use
I am *drowning*
I don't want one of their blood-money flats
or their flying prosthetic devices!
I just want to go home!
A woman screaming in rage cuts into my thoughts.
She has a thick Glaswegian accent:
"Reeeeet. That's at. Am fackan' callin' the poleece. Git az outta heeere now!"
Another voice
Scottish again, female again.
Only this time with a meeker sounding professional tone
her voice comes from below me
I look down at the swimming pool's transparent floor
notice a fake plant adorning the corner of a reception desk

the lady is a receptionist

she's on the telephone

"I am going have to ask you to calm down or I will call security."

Glaswegian woman replies, "Fuck yeee! I want the police. Ma baby ez dying en theeere."

This scene is horrible

I am locked in a padded swimming pool cell with vacant sex workers

I feel like death

I cannot help myself

I cannot help her cause

I sob

Ban Har again tries to reassure me,

"Pete, if you pass your initiation and just keep breathing, one of these flats will be yours to keep."

"Fuck you. Fuck you all and your fucking flats! I want to go home!"

My blood boils

I want to fight him

I repeatedly punch Ban Har and his staff as hard as my body allows.

(The next thing I remember was my inner fight or flight kicking in and the sound of a symphony of alarms and bleeps which did nothing but increase my panic and desperation. In reality, I had no option now but to punch for my life, meaning that the innocent and perfectly lovely medics were victims of my physical outburst – somewhat out of character! I have since apologised to the relevant staff member/s and they were gracious enough to know and understand that this was not at all in my nature and that, thankfully, it is common for patients to display aggressive or violent outbursts!)

Ban Har begs me to 'calm down'
he commands that I must trust him
"I am *trying to help you*," he claims
paranoia and mistrust strike me deeply once again
my suspicion for these people cuts deep
I thought I had escaped them and this situation
no matter how hard I try, I cannot loosen their grip on me
I am their prisoner, once again
I find myself tugging at wires, tubes, IVs
alarms blare
again, I am tranquilised as more drugs course through my veins
into my organs
my brain.

DREAM G

Katmandu by Yusuf / Cat Stevens

I have chosen this song to reminisce about some of my childhood years spent growing up in Kathmandu, Nepal. Cat Stevens' soothing, mellow voice gives me immense comfort. The coincidental nature of this song, with its links to the dream I retell, reminds me of what a bizarre, mystifying time the pandemic was for us all, as we experienced such a shift away from our perceived norms.

I am in Nepal with Nikki and my parents
we want to adopt Nepali orphaned babies
to rescue them from being sold for slave labour, etc.
The trip is emotionally charged
we arrive at the orphanage
it is clear that the children's fate (if they remained in Nepal) would be terrible
the older children are suffering with terrible diseases
we couldn't help them
only make a donation
there was no guarantee it would reach the affected children

due to the obvious corruption that existed in the
organisation
this leaves us feeling awful prangs of guilt
which grows as we make our decision on who to rehome.
We begin to regret the mission.

(In this dream, I believed Hazel was not in our lives – we
were desperate to start some kind of family.)

We are taken on a tour through the orphanage,
it is evident that some of the older kids are being used as
slaves or worse.
I feel sickened to the core
one of the tour guides informs us of three Sherpa siblings
they are all younger than four years old
their parents had both died working in the mountains
we desperately want to help these children
something about these kids feels right for Nikki and I
we begin proceedings to take them back with us to the UK
with the support of the Nepalese Government.
Wrapped in thick, wool blankets, we cradle these
innocent infants.

(Again, in this dream I was in my hospital bed.)

I am sick in bed
unable to carry the children
so Nikki escorts my mum and dad
to see if the government vehicle has turned up
to transport us back to the city.
It is a cold, dark night
I can't help thinking of all the innocent victims

that I wanted to rescue
but I am helplessly weak in bed
nurses come to check my obs –
I hand over the Sherpa babies.
Patiently, the nurse says:
"*Pete, these are not babies, these are your hospital pillows.*"
"*Pete, do you know where you are? I think you are getting confused.*"

On reflection, this conversation was being spoken in real time and not in the dream world. I was adamant that my dream was playing out in real time and insisted that she look after the babies for me as I cried in desperation!

Bizarrely, this wasn't the only time I had asked medical staff to hold pillows thinking they were babies!

DREAM H

Redemption Song by Bob Marley

As I namecheck the great Bob Marley in the dream below, I thought it would only be apt to choose one of his most moving, beautiful songs. Themes of yearning for liberation, resilience and hope are what really resonate with me in Redemption Song.

I am aboard the train returning from London with my brother
we have been drinking
I am ill in a hospital bed (Again!)
I am in my hospital bed drunk as a sailor!
I am being monitored by the on-board medical staff
they are duly checking my stats every hour or so
as I wait for my blood pressure to be checked,
I carefully hand over what I think is my baby daughter, Hazel.

In actual fact, what I handed over was a pillow, which I had been genuinely rocking in my arms, singing Bob Marley to! Once again, the nurses patiently explained that I wasn't holding my daughter, but instead, cradling and rocking a pillow in my arms! I must have some kind of fruity imagination to conjure up such nonsense, coupled with ample mind-bending medication!

DREAM I

Disco Devil by Lee "Scratch" Perry

My path once crossed with the late, great Lee "Scratch" Perry during a gig in Manchester, where I gave him my silver necklace, which had an astronaut pendant! He responded by giving me a dozen red roses which I freeze-dried as a treasured keepsake!

A running theme of my dreams from my time in hospital is that they often concern music. At the time, I was listening to a lot of dub reggae music, having been to see the likes of Lee Scratch Perry (RIP) and Horace Andy live in concert.

I am in a New York loft apartment
I am embalming the body of Lee "Scratch" Perry
I am preserving human skin in amber-coloured oil
I surround his casket with luscious technicolour plants, jewellery
and an assortment of shiny trinkets and ornaments
I attach scale model planets from the solar system to his headwear
he resembles an Egyptian God!
An alien prince.

DREAM J

My Way by Frank Sinatra

Sinatra sings about the essence of life, celebrating the ups and downs along the way. This song is reminder for me, and perhaps for all of us, that no matter what is thrown at us, we should be the best we can and make the most of every day. After all, life is not a dress rehearsal! My aim in writing this book was to not only "fix" myself, but also to create something worthwhile out of a bad situation, hopefully "the drama of time" documented in an interesting way.

Jamaican influences continue to infiltrate my dream world, descending down a whole new rabbit hole where, for some bizarre reason, I am at a Rastafarian ceremony and it is my job to prepare and bless meat for a ceremony. This is clearly a paradox since Rastafarians follow an Ital diet prohibiting the consumption of meat!

    I am cutting and portioning meat
    with the help of a priest, we bless the life that the animal has lived (!)

Upon inspection of my work for a congregational feast
the priest is visibly furious with my efforts,

saying in no uncertain terms that the food I have
prepared is cursed!

His outburst of disapproval grows worse

his face is purple with anger

he claims that I will be cursed forever for

neglecting to follow the correct procedures to consecrate
the food!

Despite the irony of the dream, it left me in a horrible
emotional state whereby I believed everything that I was
dreaming to be real, and that I was now doomed for all time.
I believe this had further traumatic effects on my mental
condition, as I vaguely remember, once again, the nurses
trying to reassure me that I was not at a religious meats
warehouse! Despite all their efforts in trying to convince me it
wasn't happening, I just wasn't accepting it. My stubbornness
in believing my dream to be true sent me on a downward
spiral as my ordeal and battle continued in a lonely, timeless,
never-ending realm.

DREAM K

Breathless by Nick Cave and the Bad Seeds

With what little awareness I had during my whole ordeal in hospital, one thing I held very close in my mind was the necessity to try and remain as still and calm as possible, and trust God / the universe and my body to do their thing and see me through. As well as focusing on stillness, I was focused on the love I had for my wife, baby daughter, family, and friends. This, without a shadow of doubt, was what gave me the comfort, clarity, and strength to carry on and try my best to survive.

From the absurd to the exotic and back again whilst spinning into the abyss, my dreams continue to adopt an international theme.

> I am now on honeymoon with Nik in Antigua
> I am gravely ill (Travelling there in my hospital bed again!)
> we arrive and it is paradise
> turquoise-blue waters, white sandy beaches
> towering mountains adorned with vibrant greenery
> a plethora of colour and life

I take in the scenery whilst my condition deteriorates
further

I keep needing to lie down in my hospital bed

(It accompanies me seemingly in every dream I have!)

A beautiful, friendly face emerges

a local female nurse called Riel

she spots that Nikki is in distress over my current
condition

Riel offers to take us to the local hospital

but warns us that as it's getting late,

we would have to wait a while to access medical attention

my stats are at an alarming point

my drip is rapidly running out

the three of us board a minibus which takes us to the
nearest hospital

we are told the hospital is within a Four Seasons Hotel
in St. John's

we arrive at the hotel/hospital and

notice that it is full of mamas arguing

they are fighting, verbally and physically

over injuries their respective teenagers have experienced

it feels lawless and makes us edgy

the calming nature of Riel helps matters for now though

she heads into the reception area to get an idea of how
long we will have to wait –

I am feeling weaker and weaker

as my condition worsens

she comes back with a face of serious concern.

"Minimum wait time of twenty-four hours," Riel
announces with tears in her eyes.

Nikki breaks down and cries at the thought of us stranded
without any help

I feel worse as the seconds tick by

I am slipping away

Riel and Nikki are incensed at the apparent corruption at play

gangsters and supposed VIPs being seen to before anyone else

jumping queues with gunshot wounds and the like

"You have to fly back home," Riel pleads now with tears rolling down her face.

"You have to come with us, we need you, Riel, please!" Nikki begs

as the three of us hold hands in unison.

With a gentle sigh, she agrees to fly with us, having let her partner know what is happening.

Of course, we pay her for her troubles and feel safer with her in our company.

As all regular, commercial flights are fully booked

we end up on what appears to be an international cargo plane

an empty cavernous vessel with no air hostesses or hosts

we board the flight at the airport north of St. John's,

the journey goes by in a flash

I have been in a coma for its duration

I awake to see both Riel and Nikki saying goodbye to me

I am dying and soon will pass

minutes from death

I have all but given up the fight

I am in Wythenshawe Hospital

there is a dreadlocked priest with an enormous, garish, blinged-up crucifix around his neck

he asks Riel and Nikki what denomination I am from

to which they state that I am not religious

he seems unimpressed by this

but proceeds to read my last rites in a booming Evangelical voice

Riel interrupts him asking him to tone it down and adopt better bedside manner

he continues with his reading

quieter now

I am in full acceptance of my situation

my battle is over

my story has been told

I am passing and slipping away into the next room

my soul rises in the tired, worn-down hospital chapel

my body remains on the bed as my soul departs and ascends

drifts slowly upwards

the stained glass windows dance with colour beneath me

everything is OK now

all is well

I am at peace

true acceptance and surrender

love unconditional.

DREAM L

Lovesong by The Cure

This song is about a deep, emotional connection and true devotion to somebody that you love. In this dream, Nikki selflessly ushers a dying couple through their last moments together in a profound and deeply dignified way.

Nikki and I are in a padded, windowless room
I am in bed (as usual!)
there is an old couple from Middlesborough in the corner of the room
life-long companions
they epitomise and embody decades of love and dedication for each other.
They are both in hospital beds, entering the last few minutes and hours of their life
I watch on as Nikki, sitting between them both, dims the lights and holds their hands, gently.

DREAM M

When I was One (Nursery Rhyme)

I wanted to portray the maddening nightmare I was experiencing whilst in my dream state, where I was subjected to an absurd, repetitive event, played out on a constant loop, whilst on board a fictitious ferry bound for Ireland. This particular nursery rhyme is a reference to the surreal, recurring ordeal I was going through, whilst I travelled 'this way, that way, forwards, backwards, over the Irish sea'.

I am in my hospital bed again (no surprise there!)
the hospital is on a ferry bound to Ireland
outside, a heavy storm batters the ferry
my drip bags are sloshing around
a nurse brings her pet parrot onto her shift
I glance at the ceiling
there are numerous exotic birds flying around the ward
parrakeets, toucans, macaws in technicolour
a hive of activity
whilst an Atlantic storm rages outside
wild grey ocean

Nikki arrives and sits in the chair next to my bed
there are other pets too
a cat
it's prowling like a caged tiger up and down the ledge
above my bed and Nikki's chair
each time the cat struts past us,
its tail brushes the back of my neck, then Nik's
we shiver and haunch up our shoulders
spines tingling
goose pimples
it brushes its tail on the back of my neck, then Nik's
we shiver and haunch up our shoulders
spines tingling
goose pimples
it brushes its tail on the back of my neck, then Nik's
we shiver and haunch up our shoulders
spines tingling
goose pimples.

This happens on repeat for what seems like an eternity.

DREAM N

Rocket Man by Elton John

In this dream there exists a different kind of Rocket Man*! The messages in this song ring true to my struggles with illness in that, much like the protagonist in Elton John's classic, I am longing for human connection and to break free from the shackles of isolation and loneliness.*

There is a distraught Polish mother
she is with her young daughter and her teenage son, Wojcik
who has been involved in a self-inflicted accident out on a Manchester council estate
he has been riding his scooter whilst half-cut
he's into gangster rap
Wojcik is out of it and rude
extremely obnoxious, slagging off everyone in sight
he's picked up minor injuries and is still able to walk
next to their area of the ward is a quiet, respectful Pakistani family
a couple with their son and daughter

it seems the dad is ill with a chest complaint

he is dressed in a traditional kaftan and masood hat.

The Polish mother is becoming impatient with the nurses and doctors

she voices her displeasure when the Pakistani family are seen to first

(they were ahead of her family in the queue)

racial slurs are fired from the mouth of Wojcik to the startled innocent family

Wojick's mum sniggers

Rod Stewart's raspy, gritty voice booms out of her tinny smartphone speaker

she is listening to *Rhythm of My Heart*

the security guard begins ushering the Polish family to a different area of the ward

they reluctantly agree

it seems as if the Pakistani dad needs regular visits to the john

the shared bathroom is located next to the Polish family's new spot

each time he visits the toilet he coughs up his guts in the cubicle

Wojcik continues with his xenophobic jeers towards the father and his family

the Pakistani dad has heard enough

he spits what looks and sounds like firecrackers onto the floor

booming bangs and crashes

this only stokes Wojcik's fire further

leading him to use derogatory sexual remarks about the man's wife and daughter

tension runs high

the Pakistani man remarks that Wojcik's dad is not around because
he's 'probably in jail serving a long sentence'.
This comment touches a raw nerve in Wojcik's mum
who shouts more insults about the colour of their skin
I take it upon myself to hop out of bed (on one leg!)
to read books to the two Polish and Pakistani daughters
attempting to diffuse the toxic situation unfolding.

POST-COMA

Landslide by Fleetwood Mac

Suddenly, I found myself awake again following my coma, which was a big relief, yet simultaneously extremely disconcerting for me, not knowing what had happened to me or, in fact, who I was! Landslide *describes the sudden and uncontrollable changes that can shift the landscape of your life.*

I have been *asleep* for thirteen days.
I was *put* to sleep in late 2020 and now,
as the doctors attempt to awaken me, it is 2021.
I went to sleep in 2020. I am waking up in 2021.
The problem is the intense delirium, extreme paranoia, and utter confusion about –
who I am
where I am and
why I am here in hospital
instead of with my girls at home hibernating through a winter lockdown.
That's the *slight* problem.
The *major* problem (as the doctors try to bring me round from my coma)

is that my flight and or fight instincts surface again, somewhat rapidly. The fact that I am a one-legged man in a hospital bed surrounded by and attached to multiple tubes means that I'm not going to press the *flight* button – there's only one thing for it.

Once again, I punch the proverbial *fight* button.

Uncharacteristically, I swipe for the doctor who is trying to save my life with a clenched fist

I scream obscenities at the nurses

this is *not* me.

I don't like this person

I have been hijacked

quickly and composed, I am restrained and predictably given *more drugs* to keep me calm and safe.

Looking back on this, I feel ashamed of my behaviour towards the medical staff, sacrificing their time on the front line as our country and the rest of the world wrestled with this hideous virus. At the same time, I understand that I was in survival mode and didn't know of any other option but to kick up a storm in that moment. I hope the doctor and nurses forgive me. In fact, according to Nikki they said they have experienced patients doing 'a lot worse'. I wonder what that could entail?!

Finally, I am awake and not comatose.

The nurses tell me I am ready to move on to a less intensive ward now that I require less critical care. I think by this point I have been in at least three or four different beds in various parts of Wythenshawe Hospital.

What was it like to wake up from a coma? It was like I was a different person. I felt like an old man, extremely frail for losing 10kg in body weight. I even sounded ancient, according to Nikki! It's funny looking back on it but upsetting at the time for everyone who knew me. Of course, my voice sounded elderly due to the tubes and pipes that went down my throat in the ventilation process. I felt old mentally as well. I was struggling to remember a lot of basic things about my life and the people around me. The confusion was *real* and *terrifying*.

It was impossible to separate the lucid dreams and nightmares from reality. I believed I was somewhere that I wasn't. I hallucinated regularly. I recall looking down at a picture of a man's face on a *MOJO* magazine beside my bed – some rock 'n' roll musician. His face started moving. Lips and eyes speaking to me but no sound coming out. I thought I was losing my mind. Maybe I was? I looked away, and then back at the face again. The guy's face continued to talk at me with no sound. What world have I woken up into? Certainly not the same one as before. *Fix me, somebody, fix me quick*, I thought to myself.

More trippy happenings occurred once I was given my phone back. I clicked on a video message from my friend, Tom. What I thought I saw was him taking a golf swing, thwacking the little white ball off a tiny sandy island in the middle of a tropical sea. In reality, he was taking his swing at the ball from a snowy, icy driving range stood on top of artificial grass. To this day, I can honestly say it looked like he was at a driving range in the Maldives!

AWAKE

Awake by Jim Morrison and The Doors

And just like that, the dreams stopped. The nightmares ceased but only to leave my brain severely confused, now in the reality of the Pulmonary Oncology Unit, as the delirium continued to present itself in new and disconcerting ways.

I am on the POU (Pulmonary Oncology Unit) ward
these days and nights are long and seemingly endless
all I want to do is sleep
my ears ring loudly
tinnitus *off the scale*
no interest in TV, phone, music
when I do sleep, it is weird
when I am awake, it is weird
the plains of consciousness that I surf are very much in-between worlds
neither reality nor fiction
I experience an almost purgatory existence
I wrestle to rediscover who and where I was before all this mess
it is upsetting.

Many people in the months after recovering have asked me, "Did it feel like you were asleep for ages? Or more like a few minutes?"

The truth is that the concept of time seemed to vanish before my eyes, nothing seemed real. I vaguely remember being in great discomfort, feeling like my lungs were being pumped up by one of those car tyre inflators – repeatedly. I also sort of recall certain staff sitting next to me with their eyes tightly glued on computer screens and messing with the settings. The rest was just a black hole of dreams. Ascending and descending into realms I had never encountered before.

I am now 'awake' since being put in an induced coma. There was yet more trauma to come as I tried helplessly to piece together the infinite jigsaw puzzle of my brain, which had been shattered and scattered into shards of immense trickery and confusion. Not to mention my pale frame having lost over 10kg in body mass. I was the worst physical and mental version of myself, and I needed repairing! (Evidently, I also needed grooming, having seen a crazed selfie that I took shortly after I woke up! My beard was out of control!)

It seems as if I have woken up and been spat out into the Guantanamo Bay Sanatorium

judging by the bright orange pyjamas the inmates are wearing –

including me

the drugs in my system mean that I find this hilarious

I start laughing manically

the laughing intensifies when I realise the guy opposite me resembles a serial killer

I study him for a while trying to make it less obvious that I am laughing

I notice he writes a lot on a pad and paper
my mind concludes he is a retired university lecturer.
To my right lies another orange PJ-suited guy
a vocal Mancunian guy in his fifties
he regularly causes trouble with the nurses, complaining about almost everything
he often leers over the younger, prettier nurses
they take offence to this
and tell him in no uncertain terms to rein it in
and to let them do their jobs
he then begins to tell me of a prospective lover
apparently he has encountered her at his local Tesco supermarket
he is intent on asking her out on a date once discharged
I encourage him to 'go for it' and ask to borrow a razor
he says he will ask her out and
kindly offers me one of his disposable BIC razors (also orange coloured!)
unfortunately, neither of us have the ability to limp across the ward room to retrieve said razor
I ask the nurse to fetch it –
only to be told that due to hygiene issues (aaah yes, global pandemic),
I wasn't allowed to use it and instead, would have to make do with an NHS-issued one.

WHERE IS MY MIND?

Where Is My Mind? by Pixies

Where was my mind? Where had it gone? I didn't know then, and I still don't know to this day!

Paranoia and suspicion brim within me as the nurses try to track down my mobile phone (my portal to home, loved ones and the outside world).

The nurses are rushed off their feet and short-staffed

they are finding it difficult to track down my phone and wedding ring

I have now been on around five wards since I first arrived in A&E two weeks ago

I don't believe that they can't locate it

I decide that the 'sinister' doctors that I encountered in my dream,

with their 'ulterior motives', have taken it from me

when I finally do get my phone, I do not trust that it is mine

in fact, I firmly believe it isn't

I am having a hard time using the phone –

reading and writing messages feels impossible due to my feeble state

this frustrates me a great deal adding to my misery

I start believing that my phone needs unlocking

I announce to the nursing staff:

"I can just walk into Bowness to get it unlocked at the phone shop."

I receive a puzzled look as they ask:

"Pete, do you know where you are?"

Firmly, I respond with, "Yeh, we're in Bowness in the Lake District. I know a mobile phone shop. The walk would be good for my physio rehabilitation."

Patiently, they respond, "Pete, you've been seriously ill, and you are in Wythenshawe Hospital."

It is now that I realise that my head is pickled from whatever the medics have done to keep me alive over the last thirteen days.

My brain lets me down again when the occupational health visitor comes to see me

her visit is welcomed as an indication that I will be out of here soon

she asks me questions about my job and home set-up

when she asks me about our bathroom, my mind goes blank

my memory freezes and I cannot, for the life of me, remember:

do we have an over-bath shower? Or a walk-in one?

I pretend to recall details of our bathroom and find myself describing our old bathroom from when we lived in Birmingham some six years previous.

Later, a group of student trainee doctors visit, surrounding my bed holding clip boards they question me about my diagnosis and health history. The whole encounter lasts around fifteen minutes

it feels like I'm being interrogated

as I answer their never-ending questions, I find myself growing utterly exhausted

I need to shut my eyes.

A few days later, still waiting on a discharge date,

a different set of trainee medics come and ask me the same questions.

Once again, I am spent.

Unbelievably, a third group of student doctors swing open my bed curtains, only this time I tell them that I have already answered the questions twice and that I didn't have the minerals to be able to go through it again.

They were very kind and understanding.

I am clearly mentally ruffled and request that Nikki brings me some more clothes. Looking back, I was in desperate need of my wife for emotional and mental support. Unfortunately, the hospital regulations hadn't changed, and visitors were still understandably forbidden to visit. This was very tough for me to take as I was in a very fragile state physically, mentally and emotionally.

Confusion was still at an all-time high when I declared to the nurses that my sister, Lizzie, was to bring a bag of clothes for me. On the phone, Nikki calmly and gently reminded me that Lizzie was thousands of miles away in Cambodia and wouldn't be in a taxi on her way to Wythenshawe Hospital with fresh clothes for me. Another tough, humiliating pill to swallow, although amusing, now, to look back on!

1.TAKEN AROUND THE RELEASE OF INEGO'S DEBUT ALBUM, DEPARTURES, 1ST OCTOBER 2020

2.HAZEL SAT AT MY PARENT'S DINING TABLE, 7 DAYS BEFORE I WAS HOSPITALISED, 20TH DECEMBER 2020

3.MARTIN AND I ON THAT FATEFUL DAY IN KINGS HEATH, 23RD DECEMBER 2020

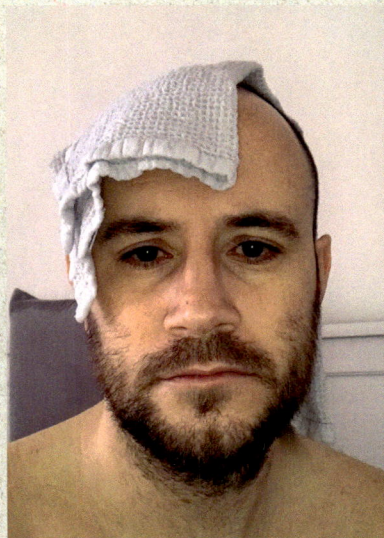

4.'IN THE DEPTHS' BEFORE B4ING ADMITTED TO A&E, 27TH DECEMBER 2020

5. THE BRIGHT LIGHTS OF WYTHENSHAWE HOSPITAL. NOTHING MY WATERMELON EYE MASK COULDN'T BLOCK OUT, WHILST SUFFERING FROM AN EYE INFECTION! 27TH DECEMBER 2020

6. FACETIME CALL WITH HAZEL, NOT LONG AFTER COMING OUT OF MY COMA, 19TH JANUARY 2021

Hsgsuwyeyw 12:54 PM

YEEOWW 12:55 PM

In BOWNESE!!!! 1:05 PM

Fantastic to hear from you lad!!!! 1:09 PM

7. WHATSAPP MESSAGES / GIBBERISH WITH TOM - CONVINCED THAT I WAS IN BOWNESS-ON-WINDERMERE, DESPITE STILL BEING A PATIENT IN HOSPITAL, 12TH JANUARY 2021

Forgot to say that the way you handled that crisis the other day with the frail couple was nothing short of amazing. You brought so much light to their ending moments nik love you 😍 5:06 PM

Like An a angel sent from heaven x 5:09 PM

8. WHATSAPP MESSAGES WITH NIKKI - ME HEAPING PRAISE FOR HER HANDLING OF THE IMAGINED PASSING OF A FICTITIOUS ELDERLY COUPLE DURING THEIR FINAL MOMENTS IN HOSPITAL! 15TH JANUARY 2021

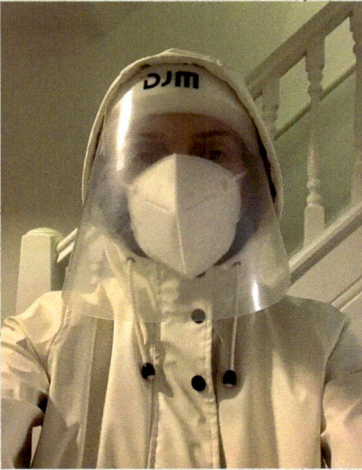

9.NIKKI, AKA THE
BEEKEEPER OF URMSTON,
KEEPING COVID-19 AT BAY,
JANUARY 2021

10. THE SUN WILL SHINE
AGAIN. TAKEN FROM MY
ISOLATION ROOM AT HOME
AFTER MY LONG AWAITED
DISCHARGE FROM HOSPITAL,
25TH JANUARY 2021

YOU'RE
DOING
PRETTY
WELL
GIVEN
THE
CIRCUMSTANCES

11. AN APT BIT OF SIGNAGE
SPOTTED IN MANCHESTER
CITY CENTRE,
1ST MARCH 2021

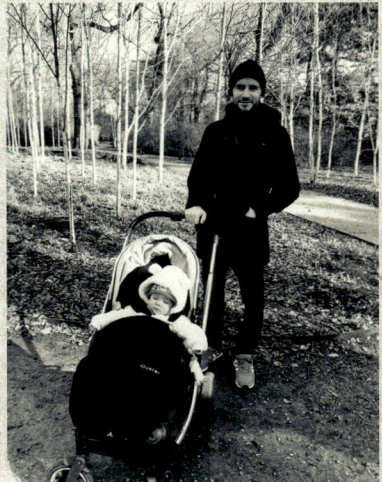

12. RECOVERY WALK,
DUNHAM MASSEY,
25TH FEBRUARY 2021

13. WHEN PETE MET STEVE! POST-LOCKDOWN, SPRING 2021

14. A PIRATE BY THE SEA, DEVON, 11TH AUGUST 2021

15. FAMILY. POLLENÇA, MAJORCA (OUR HAPPY PLACE), 26TH AUGUST 2021

16. THE CEREMONIAL BURNING OF MY MEDICAL NOTES! 19TH MAY 2024

CRUSH

Hey Porter by Johnny Cash

I desperately needed to break myself free from my perpetual state of confusion, as I yearned to know how much longer I had to endure before I could make my way back home – whatever home meant at this point in my journey, where I knew nothing about reality.

Having gained access to my phone again
I try to summon the energy required to catch up on all of my messages
but this is proving difficult
I can manage to read about three or four WhatsApp messages of goodwill
before needing to flop back down on my bed, struggling to breathe, with my eyes closed again.
All I want to do is sleep
when I am awake, my mind continues to play tricks on me.
My mind is fragile and gullible
so gullible, in fact, that I believe that one of the hospital caterers

(a tall, timid Caribbean fella with a slender physique and braided hair)

has the hots for one of the younger female nurses.

My brain convinces me that the pair of them are designing the patients' menu

coming up with names for each dish

desserts are given mushy monikers akin to 1980s Valentine's Day menus.

'Sponge cake and custard' renamed 'Blind Love'!

To which the female nurse reacts coyly, donning a melodramatic blush

fanning her face with her hand!

Of course, this was, again, complete fiction, a further sign to me that my scrambled jigsaw puzzle mind needed piecing back together!

THE END IS NIGH

Spread your Love by Black Rebel Motorcycle Club

I chose this song to highlight the sheer generosity of the staff who were helping me get back on my feet (foot!). The physio's ever constant encouragement fuelled and accelerated my recovery until I could finally be deemed medically safe and fit enough to make my long-awaited return home, back to my girls. The love and kindness I received from the care of all the staff in hospital was something to behold, spreading the right kind of virus – working so hard, serving others.

Physios force me out of bed to determine whether or not
I'm mobile enough to 'get around' and be safe at home.
A sign that my hospital stay is finally coming to an end
they bring me a Zimmer frame.
A Zimmer frame at thirty-five years of age?
That wasn't in the script!
No stranger to a mobility aid or three, I feebly click on
my prosthetic leg
and hoist myself (with difficulty), gripping the handles
of the Zimmer –

my bony, pale hands tremble from the mild exertion.

This is the most I have moved my body since my admission

apart from attempting to physically attack the medics!

I am acutely aware that this whole scene is a test

a test to decide if I can be discharged.

Failing this test simply was not an option.

The friendly young physio studies my movements

as I slowly shuffle across the ward floor

offering words of encouragement like

'you've got this, Pete' and 'nice work, mate'.

My task is to walk from one end of the room to the other, unaided –

except for the Zimmer frame, of course.

Mustering the little energy I can,

I put every ounce of my focus into this task

I've done it!

This feels like the biggest achievement of my life

I was going home

at last!

Home to my girls again.

However, I was still fighting Covid and still very infectious! (having tested positive a few days after extubation) I guess this was another reason they wanted me out of the hospital to control the spread. The Covid posed a very serious challenge once I was home with Nikki and Hazel. With the rules set out by the government very clear, we would not legally be allowed to have visitors. There would be no relief for Nikki from looking after Hazel and me! Her frail thirty-five-year-old husband bed-bound, looking and sounding like an eighty-year-old man!

THE MOMENT CAME AT LAST

You Only Get What You Give by New Radicals

Finally, I was to make my return home. Cue palpable, overwhelming relief and gratitude to have survived through it all. And now was the time to start living again.

Nurses arrive at my bed to inform me
the ambulance is on its way to take me home.
I feel an elation I have never experienced before.
I would jump for joy if I had the energy
hours pass by again
day turns into night
the Manchester skies grow darker
but out of nowhere…
two green-uniformed angels appear and announce:
"Right, let's get you home, pal."
The kind souls in green buy me a drink from the vending machine
I gladly accept a full fat bottle of Coke.
Energy.
I offer them money and they tell me there's no need

they say that I had been through enough and it was the least I deserved.

Kindness is still alive
pass it on
the right kind of virus.

HOME

Head Underwater by Jenny Lewis

One of my all-time favourites – a magical song about survival, resilience, and the will to keep going, no matter what life throws at you. A reminder that there is always some sand left in the hourglass.

Back home I start to feel the old me coming back
I cannot hug Nikki and Hazel
this hurts and feels unnatural
I try to comfort myself
The embraces will feel all the sweeter when they're finally allowed.
I shouldn't laugh but do
Nikki steps into the spare bedroom where I am quarantined
she is dressed as what can only be described as a demented bee-keeper
decked out head to toe in PPE
Nikki is a saint for what she's had to endure
looking after a nine-month-old baby

whilst her husband flirts with death on a machine in hospital

she is a warrior

I crave pancakes all the time

I crave junk food

I need five meals a day

I am 10kg lighter

I am grateful for my parents who visit us from afar

they drop off delicious home-cooked meals –

fish pies, fresh curries, lasagne

I am in heaven after three weeks of hospital food

my parents' visits are strange affairs

They are more like doorstep deliveries

They deliver meals to Nikki across the threshold

Their faces concealed by masks

keeping their distance

I have missed my mum and dad and hate that, after weeks of solitude,

I must wave down at them from the guest bedroom upstairs

I see them wrapped up in coats and scarves

stood outside in our garden

in the cold

I feel warmth but also sadness

questions pop into my head like:

what have *they* had to go through?

Their youngest son gravely ill *again*

this time they've been forbidden to visit and give me support

will this make us all stronger?

Time will tell.

These are strange days for our family

for families across the country

the world

we try and master the art of social distancing

when you're living in each other's pocket, that becomes almost impossible

despite Nikki's best efforts to steer clear of the dreaded Covid

Hazel, our precious daughter, tests positive

thankfully, after initial concern, she doesn't seem to experience severe symptoms

still, it is heartbreaking hearing her cough almost continuously for days.

Her tiny lungs are working too hard

I feel personally responsible

I've been chewed up and spat out of hospital and back home

to infect my family

we are, as Jim Morrison put it, 'riders on the storm'.

One day, we will look back at this episode of our lives

and marvel at how strong we all were

our resilience turned up to eleven.

REST AND REHAB

Slipstream by Strand of Oaks

Timothy Showalter, amongst a backdrop of surrealist lyrics, sings about his yearning for human connection and human touch. I had spent around three weeks in isolation. Still infected with Covid, I was then sent home. This meant I had to be isolated from my family for several days, unable to hug and physically connect with my wife and daughter. The need to hold them and feel their touch, after such a traumatic time, was overwhelming for me – so hard to bear.

I have been home for over a week
my days consist of resting and practising walking with my frame
I am desperate for a *long, hot shower*
(*I had to endure bed washes the whole time at Wythenshawe!*).
The steam irritates my cough
makes it hard to breathe
this drives Nikki mad with worry considering what I have just been through

once my coughing fits subside,

the sensation of hot water hitting my back and skin is a healing and joyful experience

the little things we take for granted

a shower and a comfy bed.

The days that follow involve the three of us

reconnecting as a family

making up for lost time

it feels unnatural to us to be refraining from human touch

I am desperate to do playtime with Hazel

be her daddy again

but I'm still contagious with Covid

Nikki and I continue to wear masks at all times

strange days in the modern world.

Days turn into weeks

weeks into months

Hazel's Covid passes,

passes onto Nikki.

How much more can we take of this?

Nik's symptoms are different

she presents with awful sinus pain and migraines

our family is being pushed to our limits physically, mentally and emotionally

we are in dire need of help but we cannot get it

we have been quarantined for weeks, months even

surely any future cards we are dealt will be nothing compared to this?

SEASONS CHANGE

Winter by The Rolling Stones

The hardest of winters was finally showing signs of passing. The longest, most arduous winter months I and many others had ever faced. Signs of spring were now emerging, like a miracle. Just around the corner, the promise of summer sun would hopefully heal us all of what we'd collectively been through.

We find ourselves transported from winter to spring
the dark, cold nights fade
swapping short, painful days with the hope of spring
a new chapter to look forward to
hope that this damned pandemic will ease
hope that we'll be reconnected with family, friends,
music – being *together again*
take our lives off pause
that's what the whole world hopes for
a collective dream.
Boris allows us to meet up with loved ones outdoors
we meet with my parents in a Cheshire park
we see deer and shoots of new daffodils

yesterday's gone
yesterday has indeed gone but it's left quite a mark
my body is still frail and weak
I still lose my breath from daily tasks
my only focus is to get myself strong again
both physically and mentally
I dedicate much of my time into a gruelling physio regime
For my mental well-being I sign myself up for counselling
to try and fix the wreckage of my brain!
All this sounds very purposeful, doesn't it?
Though there is one *slight problem.*
I am beginning to experience terrible toothache
my mouth is throbbing intermittently.

I laugh writing this because you just could not make the
next bit up.

DESTINED FOR THE DENTIST

Your Teeth in My Neck by Scientist

Just when I thought things were looking up again, unexpectedly, arrived another of my medical downfalls (!) to endure, which left us no choice but to laugh as I suffered excruciating discomfort in my teeth and gums, probably due to the intubation. The subsequent visits to the dentist inflicted considerable pain both to my mouth and wallet!

I struggle to my car in my Zimmer frame
this is hilarious
it's important to laugh and revel in my downfall!
My joints tremble
my skeletal hands shake in the blustery February winds
I am on my way to the *dentist.*
For the past couple of weeks I have been reliant on painkillers for the toothache
I take the maximum dose to ease the immense pain.
In the dentist waiting room, the lady behind the desk reassures me
my appointment will take place on the ground floor

I am a young dude rocking a Zimmer, remember?!

I plonk myself down onto a chair

panting into my surgical mask

my lungs are working hard. Again.

Leave us alone, they plead to me.

Nadia, my lovely Iranian dentist, calls me into the room

her smile would light up a stage

a smile so welcome in these bleak, uncertain times

although she has a *serious* mask on, I notice the warm crinkle of her eyes as they light up

she says something like:

"My God, Pete, you've been through a lot, haven't you?"

She inspects my mouth with the usual metal implements

I begin to clock a tool that I haven't seen before

a small, gleaming, silver hammer

despite its size, it looks as though it could do some damage

I wince.

I cower like a street dog.

"Just lift your arm up if it hurts," Nadia reassures.

Her blue-gloved hand clutches the weapon

ah yes, the blue gloves, I know you so well

she starts tapping away at my front teeth which I can cope with

as she moves around my mouth, I tremble in fear

knock knock, *tap tap*

before getting a chance to raise my arm, I let out a guttural wail.

"*Aaaaaarggghhhhhhhh*," I scream, nearly pushing my friendly dentist over.

Nadia looks concerned and suggests she does an X-ray of my teeth

try and figure out what is causing so much pain

Nadia prepares the X-ray device.

"Could you tap your feet together?" is what I hear her ask me.

As requested, I begin repeatedly tapping my feet together
Nadia and her hygienist look on bemused
I notice Nadia's face turning bright red
she has laughing eyes
she attempts to correct what I misheard:
"No, no. I said, tap your *teeth* together!"

Mortified, I utter the sorry words, "Well, I am at the dentist, after all, aren't I?"

My deafness had failed me this time.

I was to return to see Nadia in a few days once the results of the scan had been processed.

When I told Nikki about 'Hammer Gate' and my hilarious feet clapping, we couldn't help but laugh
in hysterics, laughing at our calamitous journey.

During the wait for the results, I throw myself into my physio regime
I continue to enjoy five meals a day (with snacks in between, of course!)
in a bid to regain the lost weight
around this time, we also enjoy something that you simply cannot put a price on
– *a hug.*

A long-awaited Hazel hug
I cry tears of joy as I wrap my baby girl in my arms
I will never forget that first embrace
nowadays, we make a ritual of our precious family hug.
Results day arrives fast
once again, I drive to discover my fate at the dentist
as I enter the room to see Nadia, she is glancing over the results of my X-ray

the news is not good

of course it isn't, why would it be any different?

"You have an exposed nerve which needs an immediate root canal followed by a crown days after. Oh, and one other thing, your existing fillings need *re-doing* as they have been somewhat dislodged," Nadia apologetically announces.

Bombshell.

My thoughts focus on the pain

I mull over the ordeal that I'll have to endure for Nadia to fix my mouth

and the misery these procedures will inflict on my bank balance

paying for torture.

Sigh.

Call Nikki. Break news. Laugh. *Laugh hysterically. Cry maybe.*

Over the next few weeks, I return to Nadia for my treatments

each time feeling a little bit stronger and more repaired

this is a good thing.

A barometer for my healing.

I have a healed future to believe in.

Nikki and I continue to find humour in this whole ordeal

could you even make it up?

In life, I believe that with every bad bit of news, there is something precious or good attached to it

this next part was one of those moments.

Even after the treatment, the pain in my mouth continues to bother me

in desperation, I seek help from my GP

he suggests that I try a steroid nasal spray

he believes the spray will target my sinus areas which are linked to the mouth worth a shot, eh?

I start the course of steroids

within days, the pain that I was living with pretty much *vanished*

look how good it gets if you just hold on!

(Although I had spent a lot of money on dental treatments, I'm fairly certain I can say that I never bemoaned the cost. I was simply so relieved to have found a cure for this awful pain and grateful to not have to take painkillers all the time.) I am ultimately so thankful to my GP, Dr G, for solving this problem for me. In hindsight, perhaps my teeth were messed up and neglected after such invasive action in hospital.

'NORMAL' LIFE

Medicine by Inego

Some of the best moments and memories of my life have been as drummer with our band Inego. I am so proud of our brotherhood and what we have managed to achieve over those years: seeing our first vinyl EP end up on the shelves of Manchester's HMV store; crowdfunding, then recording our debut album at the legendary Magic Garden Studios with the sonic wizard / guru, Gavin Monaghan; countless gigs up and down the country and even overseas.

I distinctly remember waking up from my coma with almost unbearable tinnitus – the constant sound of a swarm of locusts inside my head. Even wearing ear protection, the impact of the drums spiked these symptoms, significantly affecting my sleep, everyday life and work. This unfortunately led me to the difficult decision to retire from drumming. Despite hanging up my drumsticks, I am proud to still be a part of the band in some capacity, such as providing occasional backing vocals, and who knows when they will find a cure for tinnitus in the future?

During the weeks that follow

I slowly reintegrate myself back into *normal* life

whatever that means

I have become interested in people's perception of the whole ordeal.

Not just what I had to go through…

but also what my family and friends had to go through

I notice a common theme is that some say:

"You've been so unlucky. Cancer and now this."

Granted, I have been through a lot, maybe more than most

but I certainly don't feel that I have been unlucky

quite the opposite, in fact.

I feel, given what I *have been through*,

I am incredibly lucky and fortunate to be still here today

typing away on my laptop.

Still alive, still breathing

waking up, against all odds, to see another day

this fills me with enormous grace and gratitude for the *gift of life*

I would never wish the cancer, becoming an amputee or pneumonia and sepsis on anybody

but the immense joy found in overcoming such challenges,

I hope all people feel that type of joy.

It is true as I sit here today writing this

there are still challenges

the ringing in my ears (tinnitus) is fighting for my attention

taking over my focus and concentration

I have had to make changes (drastic ones) because of my tinnitus

For starters, I have had to retire from drumming –
not a decision taken lightly after fourteen glorious years
behind the kit
providing beats for our band, Inego
it's time for a new era to begin
whatever that is, I really don't know
but I am *so relieved* to have survived
to be with my girls every day is the ultimate blessing
to be able to see the seasons changing
I am able to go on holiday, go to gigs, football matches,
meet up with friends, laugh and party
what a gift
it was all so very close to being taken away from me.
I know that.

THE RETURN VISIT

Sleeping In by The Postal Service

I remember discovering this song soon after I had woken from the coma, when I was completely losing my mind in a distant hospital wing, so far away from life as I once knew it. Headphones in, I let the music wash over me as the words and the sounds made me cry tears of relief and sadness – sadness at the predicament we had all faced, relief to have somehow got out of it alive by the skin of my teeth. At this point in my journey, my circadian rhythms all over the place, I found sleep very hard to come by. This was so exhausting, because all I wanted to do was sleep and sleep after fighting hard for so long.

On the 24th of May 2021, months after my discharge, I returned to one of the wards (POU) where I was treated, where my confusion was at a maximum, having recently come round from my coma. I had a burning desire to return to where I had experienced such high levels of delirium and trauma. This yearning to 'go back' might sound like a bizarre move, but I needed to return, as I thought this would aid my recovery. I thought it would be therapeutic to see, hear and smell the place where I was a post-ICU coma patient, in order to close that particular chapter for good.

I arrive at Wythenshawe Hospital –
a bittersweet place
a place that I never want to go back to after today
but also a joyous place that brought the safe arrival of our daughter, Hazel
a place that, let's remember, *kept me alive.*
I shuffle through the corridors towards the POU ward
the ward is at the arse-end of the hospital
the nether reaches.
I meet with Kim, the ward manager
she has kindly agreed to show me around today
in our initial chat in her office
we discuss the whole ordeal
what myself and my family have gone through and the pandemic in general
the tone is serious when out of the corner of my eye,
I notice a bright *pink penis pen* sticking out of Kim's stationary pot!
I hold in my laughter and try to refocus on our conversation.
Comic relief indeed!
Kim explains how ICU staff would've told me that I had to be intubated
along with all of the associated risks
tubes down my throat, etc.
Ventilation
placed in an induced coma
the risks

Kim explains that I may've had to sign a disclaimer (or issue a verbal disclaimer)

to agree for the coma to proceed

knowing that this approach could cause danger to life.

I am escorted through the Pulmonary Oncology Unit into Room 1

the very room I was situated as a patient

the exact room where I knocked a whole jug of water on the floor

whilst attempting to hop on one leg to the toilet!

This event got me in trouble with the nurses as one yelled,

"If you slipped and broke a bone, we wouldn't be insured."

I realised my mistake but felt in this instance their bedside manner was lacking

the reason I had got out of bed is because nobody had answered my call for over twenty-five minutes

this was a far cry compared to previous wards I was cared for on

I put it down to staff being overworked, underpaid and understaffed

despite this, not a nice way of being treated, especially when clinically confused!

Room 1 brings back other undesirable memories

one thing I found particularly frustrating

was not being permitted to use the ensuite shower due to lack of staff

and the number of nurses (two) that would be needed to assist me with this

despite my insistence that I could shower myself,

they would not back down

(on reflection, probably rightly so considering my condition, lack of physical strength and lung capacity!).

I do remember sleep being very hard to come by in this room

I put this down to discomfort, drugs and the perpetual ringing in my ears

I definitely notice the tinnitus became worse after waking from the coma.

Because of the insomnia, I distinctly remember experiencing hallucinations.

ROOM ONE HALLUCINATIONS

Your Arms Around Me by Jens Lekman

After some recovery at home, I had a burning desire to return to the ward where I remember suffering from hallucinations and delirium the most. I felt compelled to make sense out of all the confusion and be reorientated to reality, time, and space. I hoped this would help in fixing up my brain as it reassembled itself, slowly organising and separating fiction from reality.

> *Work colleagues' cars drive past my window,*
> *an Italian father talks of paninis*
> *the food he will eat when he gets home*
> *a footballer and his family are staying in my room*
> *early check-out for a transatlantic flight to Florida*
> *faces contort, garish foam masks*
> *nasty nurses with vendettas*
> *brimming paranoia.*
> *Are they talking about me?*
> *Why are they laughing?*
> *Am I dead?*
> *There is a leak in the ceiling*

drip drip drip
rusty surroundings.
Workers fix an extractor.
I am in an empty stadium
bands in a recording session
on a boat bound for Ireland
I am not in control
I am the subject of a twisted video game
I must be free
I must be freed.
Will I ever make sense of it all?

At what point did I dream what? Where was I physically when I travelled to these stories?

Time must heal me
like it has done before.
Time will heal me
like it has done before.
Time will heal us
like it has done before
Look how good it gets if you just hold on.

HOSPITAL REFLECTIONS

Broken Radio by Jesse Malin

I couldn't choose a list of songs without including my all-time favourite artist, Jesse Malin. I have seen Jesse live countless times through the years, across various cities, from Manchester to London, to Dublin, to New York.

Jesse will always be a friend and hero of mine, having been so kind to me, my family, and friends down the years. On our trip to NYC, he welcomed me and my friends into his East Village bar. Most notably, he even wrote a song for me in 2009, as I went through bone cancer treatment as a young man.

I have become a dedicated supporter of his music and message of PMA (positive mental attitude). Just like I did, I hope and pray Jesse will return like a phoenix from his own recent health battles. I cannot wait for his long-awaited return to the stage, back where he belongs!

I sit in my car and stare up at the looming hospital building

I am crying

it's a beautiful summer's day –
trees blowing in the sweet breeze
blue skies now
grey skies then
I glance up towards the ward where Hazel was born
tears of sadness are replaced by a smile of contentment
I am slightly broken but I am alive
that's *all* that matters
the parts that are broken
I intend to fix bit by bit.
It wasn't my time.
Kim tells me I am lucky to be alive
she encourages me to put my nightmares in a 'box' and
move on.

EPILOGUE

The Rising by Bruce Springsteen

This song captures the spirit and sacrifice made by front line workers, the real unsung heroes the world over, particularly in times of crisis. Originally written after 9/11 in New York, it resonates just as much power and emotion decades later.

What I experienced across my three-week stay in the Covid winter of 2020/21 was some of the loneliest times of my life. I am acutely aware that many millions of individuals and their families across the world went through very similar journeys. Some were not as lucky as I was to survive, and I dedicate this book to those people and their families' plight as the world tried to tackle and make sense of a horrendous and challenging time across the globe. I would also like to dedicate this piece of writing to all of the frontline key workers who selflessly sacrificed their time and risked their lives whilst trying to serve others.

So where am I at now? Where is my head? As I currently write this epilogue, it is three and a half years since my discharge from hospital. I am proud of my recovery, my rehabilitation and all that has happened since. Dealing with the trauma is no mean feat, but I feel I have used my suffering and my story to create something that may help others and produced a deeply personal record from an unprecedented time in the history of the world.

It may sound as if I have 'fixed myself' which one consultant stated I had done, upon hearing about me attending talking therapy sessions, physio and indeed this cathartic writing journey. Despite this claim, I appreciate that there is still a degree of mental and emotional processing yet to do. I recognise that I may never fully understand what happened or why it happened, but I have always really valued the resource of talking therapy and believe it can work wonders on any individual if they are willing to put in the 'hard yards' before reaping the benefits. Finally, I feel that with every negative or catastrophic event, there is always light, hope and positivity that comes after it.

I know life is not a dress rehearsal, and as our friend Gavin says about our short time on earth 'we're only here five minutes'. Life is a gift and so with this in mind, I am committed to making the most out of each day I am granted, and I look forward to what is next, knowing that I am stronger and wiser than before. I am not done yet and there is so much I want to see, learn and do with my little family.

LIFE IS A POINT OF VIEW

In Reverse by The War on Drugs

In Reverse *is a favourite of mine from this band. It is a song especially befitting to end this piece as it explores the process of navigating through life's uncertainties and challenges. It's about trying to piece together the past, whilst moving forward with positivity and optimism.*

The following contributions have been kindly written by some of my friends and family who have offered their own personal reflections on how they individually experienced the Covid winter of 2020/21 and my brush with death!

WRITTEN BY LIZZIE HODGE, MY SISTER

River by Joni Mitchell

I have always loved Joni Mitchell, but River *has a particular significance given the distance I was from Pete during this time. I so badly wanted to be there, to teach my feet to fly. The song references a recognisable Christmas tune, but played with such a melancholy tone that matched the contradiction of what is usually such a fun and positive time of the year. Joni sings of everyone enjoying Christmas, but all she wants to do is skate away.*

Whilst the rest of the world was hunkered down in their bubbles, we felt reasonably lucky that despite not being able to travel home for Christmas, we could at least travel domestically and get to our beloved Lazy Beach for Christmas spent with other stranded friends and colleagues in the same situation. Lazy Beach, on Koh Rong Samloen, an island off the mainland of Cambodia, has become a home from home destination for us, an idyllic tropical sandy beach; no roads, no Wi-Fi, totally off the grid – paradise. We felt so lucky that despite the place having temporarily closed, there were enough of us regulars who wanted to go that the owner agreed to open it for the holidays. Amazing: the whole resort to ourselves without having to share it with any randoms! To still be able to travel and make the most of being stranded... from what we heard from friends and family in the UK and on the news, we were most definitely best off there. Despite having our besties with us, our family away from home, it never felt quite right to not be sharing the excitement with cousins and siblings at this time of year... *Never mind, just feel lucky we aren't in the torrid mess that the UK is in and make the most of it...* Sunny days on the beach, kids learning to surf, snorkelling on the coral reef, cocktails, cards, seafood, epic sunsets, great company. Happy days peppered with a pinch of guilt that we somehow shouldn't be having such a great time when the rest of the world was having the shittest time ever.

A few days in, I saw Josh, the manager, come run-walking down the beach towards us... weird 'cos I never saw this guy on the beach; he was always propping up the bar looking after the restaurant. *What does he want? Why does he look so serious?* Next odd occurrence, he came to whisper something to me! I guess he thought I should be the one to hear it without having an audience. Straining to take this in, I'm stood there in my bikini in the scorching heat, sun in my eyes. He told me my mum had sent an email to the office on the mainland (remember, no Wi-Fi) to let me know that Pete is seriously ill in hospital and that I should know and get in touch as soon as possible. What the fuck? Now I retrack: he was sick leading up to Christmas, even sending comical photos of him in bed feeling as rough as a badger's arse. But hospital? Seriously ill? Thankfully, Josh then told me that he has a dongle sim thing in his bungalow that I could use but couldn't tell anyone the password (he's had Wi-Fi all these years? cheeky bastard!). It only works in their bungalow, so I sat on the steps and nervously made the call. It all felt too close to fourteen years ago. How can this be happening *again*?! Mum sounded tired and worried but was trying to stay calm. She was apologising for interrupting my holiday (please don't be sorry) but that I should be kept in touch 'cos it was that serious.

The next few days were the most excruciating, isolating days of my life. Every day I waited to hear more news. The way things were progressing, a lot could happen in twenty-four hours, so the wait was painful. The worst part (one of the worst parts) was having to wait till 3 or 4pm to get an update 'cos of the time difference. Trying to put on a brave face for my kids during the day (God, those days stretched on and on), letting them know what was happening but not too much to alarm them, letting them enjoy their holiday, going swimming with them, continuing the ping pong tournament. I was very aware that this news had put a huge cloud over the general mood of the holiday for my friends too. They, of course, were so lovely and supportive and concerned, and genuinely interested to know the updates, but I tried desperately not to let my devastation and worry take over all conversations. It was a total nightmare battling with the news, worrying constantly, holding back tears and, at the same time, trying to join in the festivities of the holiday with friends. Every day I would get an update from Mum, I think that was to the family WhatsApp group – the messages have since disappeared from my phone and so much of this time has become a trauma-riddled blur. We would collectively send out positive vibes (Pete loves the vibes!), send out messages of support to each other and repeatedly say 'come on, Pete!'. Mum would share terrifying and increasingly worse updates each day, medical updates on things like blood pressure, oxygen levels, heart rate, organ function, etc. I was oddly grateful for these factual updates; even though they scared the shit out of me, it was clear information, a way to get a sense of what was happening, to understand the gravity. I would message back and forth with Nikki, Pete's wife, everyday too. We would collectively tell him to get his shit together and get home, keep fighting, stop with the attention-seeking already, *come on, Pete*! She was at home with baby Hazel and her mum; God, I can't begin to imagine the torment of not being able to visit him. She is such a strong woman. I am so proud of how she coped with such dignity and positivity.

As the days went on and the severity continued to increase, the more I couldn't stand being in paradise. I would be stood on a patch of beach where the phone line was least glitchy, looking out at a brilliant sky full of pinks, reds, oranges, hearing the grimmest of news. It didn't feel right to be somewhere so beautiful. It felt sick, grotesque even. I wanted to go home; I was exhausted with putting on a brave face every day, worrying about ruining my friends' holidays. I just wanted to be home to process everything without everyone around, but I had to consider that this was our kids' holiday too; it would be unfair to drag them home just so I could indulge in my misery. So instead, we stuck it out. I felt stifled not to be able to let it out when I needed to, drained with the pretence of the 'holiday'. I felt so far away, so helpless. I knew that even if I could get back to the UK, I wouldn't be any good to anyone: I would have to isolate somewhere, be in the way and a burden. I also knew and weirdly took comfort in the fact that this wasn't just the case for me. We all felt distanced, even if some family were only a few miles away from him. Every night I would sit on the balcony and weep for hours and hours, finally being able to let it out, always with Matt by my side. I would imagine Pete lying there fighting for his life *on his own* without any of us to comfort him; it broke my heart. He may be a grown man but he's still my little brother. *Do you know we are with you, Pete? Are you afraid? Are you in pain?*

On the evening that I was told that he may not make it through the night (the day that Nikki was called to come in to the hospital to see him; you know it's bad when they are allowing family to come in), I couldn't find a way to process what was happening, what I had been told. Tears were not enough: I impulsively ran into the sea in the middle of the night and screamed, roared into the night sky to Pete. I wanted to somehow send him energy, let out mine, it was an uncontrollable force. The painful waiting...

He got slowly better, came round, he was awake! It's a long road to recovery from here and I was shocked at how pale and thin he looked, but he's alive and he's going to be OK. We are bloody lucky to have you continue to fill our days with joy, to entertain and annoy us still. Love you, Pete xxx

WRITTEN BY NICK HODGE, MY BROTHER

Many Rivers to Cross by Jimmy Cliff

A soulful, heartbreaking song, steeped in symbolic meaning about despair. Many Rivers to Cross *references challenges we face, but ultimately gives rise to hope. It seemed a fitting melody to soothe the spirit but also reflect on what happened to Pete and our family at the time. One of my favourite songs that evokes emotions, reflects on life and the journeys we encounter.*

Christmas 2020 promised a great deal – finally some time with friends and family. I remember looking forward to some respite from the bizarre teaching experience my family had all been through: my kids in bubbles and Nicky and I (secondary art teachers) walking from section to section in our respective schools, teaching in alien spaces and basically doing our best. Families and friends were virtual, although a strange new bond was found during this madness.

Pete and Nikki had enjoyed a whirlwind of a year. In many ways, amongst all the surreal situations they were beyond content: life was good, Hazel was perfect and still is. The joy that Hazel brought to them, and the rest of the family, almost seemed to balance the situation we were all facing. Everyone couldn't be happier for them – Hazel was a symbol of hope and certainly happiness. A miracle that shone a light in the dark.

I remember quite clearly a conversation on Christmas Eve with Pete when he said he was going to rest in the hope that he could celebrate with the rest of Nikki's family in Birmingham on Christmas Day – he was in bed feeling rough. I thought nothing of it… the update the next day was not great: Pete had to stay in bed and miss Christmas – shite for Pete. Two days later, the call came saying that Pete had been struggling with his breathing – ambulance called. What the actual fuck – how had it come to this? Mum was concerned although reassuring. The last time we were in this situation, I remember driving through the night with Lizzie (our sister) to visit Pete in hospital in Wigan twelve years previous – we had been given 'the call' as Pete had developed septicaemia. How could we be back here again?

Our world flipped again: Pete was fighting another battle. The family were in bits, although if it's possible, an even tighter bond was felt amongst us all with Pete and Nikki at the centre of all our thoughts. I felt a distance from Pete never felt before as he was locked down and shut down – an induced coma; the emotions turned to Nikki and baby Hazel. There was hope, although the daily statistics on the BBC did not help. Why was this happening again? What could we do? A helpless overwhelming feeling of frustration was felt; hours turned into days and the days turned into weeks. Emotions seemed blurred and surreal – trying to keep positive, as that is what Pete would do, and that seemed to be the only action and antidote to the situation Pete was in.

Pete came back to life! He had survived and been brought out of his induced coma. I remember feeling exhausted – the pent-up emotions surfaced; I desperately wanted to speak to my brother to know it was real. He was certainly with us, although a little confused to say the least – delirious madness had struck: he was convinced in his head of experiences beyond the norm. It didn't matter though; he was alive and that was all that mattered.

He's 'better' now, by the way, although still mad as a box of frogs! Normal Pete – back to the brilliance of Pete.

WRITTEN BY RACHEL HODGE, MY MUM

Human by The Killers

Human *sings out the deep fear I held of the thin veil between life and death I knew Pete was dancing over. The not knowing. The fragility. Looking for the answers. Hope.*

26th **December 2020 2.30pm** – You have just managed to get home. You have left family Christmas in Birmingham suddenly, feeling very ill and desperate to get home. You call me. "*I feel terrible, Mum, I'm coughing, coughing, can't get my breath... I'm so thirsty... I'm drinking a lot but I can't pee. I've tested – it's not Covid.*"

27th – I call our GP friend – she advised you should drink a lot for 2 hrs – then if no better phone 111... but next thing I hear is you are getting much, much worse and can't breathe. Coughing, fever, fast pulse...

Late afternoon – you tell Nikki you feel strange and unstable. She calls 999... you are blue lighted to A&E.

Admissions ward 28th – Nikki visits. She calls me and relates that Pete is exhausted… no sleep… sore eyes and lips… on oxygen and antibiotics… deteriorated during the day… staff expressed concern… monitoring carefully but if/when necessary, he'll go to ICU.

29th –

"Hello, I'm Pete Hodge's mum. How is he doing?"

"We are [inaudible] *worried about him."*

"Sorry – you are not *worried about him?"*

"No, we are very *worried about him. Intensive Care team are on their way to assess him."*

My stomach hits my throat… I am reeling with nausea.

Maybe 30 mins later, Pete calls… stomach hits throat.

[Weak, breathless voice.] *"I'm going to intensive care* [inaudible] *ventilator… rest."*

"Oh Pete… I'm so sorry… you'll be in the best place… it'll give your body a rest… love you love you."

I am cold, numb, desolate… I was a nurse… I know what this means… I am so afraid for Pete.

Ward Sister: *"…Need to give him a rest through induced coma and ventilation for two or three days. Pete is such a lovely young man -a real pleasure to look after."*

Admitted to ICU 29th **Dec:** This is hell… I can't see you Pete… I can't speak to you. I wish I had some feeling that I know what's going on and so fight your corner and keep you safe like I did when you were so ill with cancer. How can I trust what I can't see? I'm so afraid for you…

January 2021 – It's carnage in the NHS… I'm so frightened of human error in ICU… it can so easily happen. I know your life is on a knife edge with or without human error.

I try to keep up and share with close friends and family what is unfolding with Pete, by writing daily WhatsApp messages.

WhatsApp, 29th–31st Dec:

29th – *Pete critically ill now with sepsis.*

30th – *Some progress… but temp spiking… they are still mystified as to quite how this took hold so severely and quickly… doing many different tests… asked if he'd ever eaten wild mushrooms!!*

31st – *Feeling quite upset and anxious this morning… thinking about what Pete will have to go through… discontinue ventilation failed… temp spiking… escalated antibiotics. Sister told Nikki "to be honest it's trial and error".*

Nikki is very scared, exhausted, hustling in every way possible for Pete. She is asking me so many questions that mostly I can't answer. "Why haven't they done…? What does that mean…? Surely they should…? Could it be…? She is fighting, fighting for him each minute of every day. I can see that she believes – no, she insists – that he will pull through this. What is wrong with me, I wonder? I feel weak and guilty that I can't 'keep the faith', as Pete used to say. I honestly do not dare to think that Pete will, for sure, pull through. I think, *how can I say my child will but your child won't?* Nikki thinks I am deeply affected by witnessing the heartbreak of mothers who lost their children to cancer at the young oncology unit, Christie Hospital. To share the load, Nikki and I agree that I try to speak to a doctor every day for an update which I'll then share with her (but this just doesn't happen). It helps a lot that she can speak each day to the ICU nurses, who are such a support to her. I really envy her that she can see, kiss, touch Pete and speak to him.

One long, long day runs into another. It is a comfort for us to do all the normal rituals – wash, dress, teeth, breakfast, get wood, lay fires. Then speak to Nikki… "How was Pete last night?"… "What did the nurse say?" Then comes the anxiety… we try to understand what might be 'progress'… or 'no progress'… or, God forbid, 'getting worse'. We try to guess what the right questions might be… guess what extra tests might be needed… guess what the daily up and down results mean… guess where the medics might have missed some significant info… our two brains are boiling as we are fighting, fighting for Pete to keep alive and survive this.

WhatsApp 1st–4th January:

1st – *Mixed news… some stats not ideal so need to improve 'not ready yet… temp spiking'.*

2nd – *Most stats OK but temp spiking gradually reducing ventilation. Pm not as good. Nurse: he's young… strong but needs more time.*

3rd – *Temp up – more bloods and sputums… moved to different ICU as Covid negative and they need beds for Covid patients.*

4th – *More stable but changed antibiotic… baffled about infection. Bronchoscopy and lungs flushed. Liver function still not stable.*

Afternoons and evenings pass writing up the day's medical notes, sending updates, reading lovely messages of support from family and friends. Phone calls with our nearest are our lifeline. This does help… so much time is spent wondering… worrying… waiting. The nights: miraculously, sleep comes with emotional exhaustion… I hold on to the bedhead with one hand and Fin's shoulder with the other… this anchors me somewhat. We say little… silence speaks our hurt for Pete's suffering… our fear. I wake up crying then get up to start the day again.

Nikki's anxiety, fear, confusion is palpable but so is her sheer bloody-minded certainty that Pete will pull through. Me – my mind and body suspended in a sort of deadly calm, zombie mode – I try to comfort, reassure, build up Nikki's trust that everything possible is being done, but in truth I am on constant fearful high alert and do not dare to have too much hope in case I must face losing Pete. I feel this lack of complete faith is letting her and Pete down.

WhatsApp 5th January: *Dr told Nikki that he remains critically ill… body reacted to lowered sedation… too much discomfort with tube… so increased again. Both lungs severely infected, inflammation markers high, BP high so needs meds… infectious diseases team now involved.*

FFS sake, is it really so hard to get to speak to a doctor? Finally, after trying for days, a doctor comes to the phone:

"*Can I speak to the consultant?*"

"*Sorry, they are not available.*"

"*OK – the registrar?*"

"*Sorry, I'm afraid not.*"

"*Right – may I ask what your role is on ICU?*"

"*I'm a GP in training.*"

FFS sake – another brick wall. Such is the terrible situation in hospitals during this period, for staff trying to cope at the height of the Covid outbreak. I do feel ashamed not to have more trust – I know from Nikki how amazing and wonderful the ICU nurses are, both their skill and their compassion.

I am so worried about Nikki – I know Rita (her mum) is with her but how is she possibly managing physically, mentally, emotionally to keep on going... going... going visiting Pete, fighting for Pete, looking after baby Hazel?

A terrible day comes: the doctors tell her that if Pete gets any worse, he could die. She responds with absolute insistence and defiance, telling me she screamed to herself across the hospital car park: *"Yes he f... will pull through, yes he f... will... come on, Pete... come on."*

These were times that were clearly very dark for her. On one such day, my heart broke for her: *"We've only just got her* [Hazel]," she says so quietly, tearfully. Her and Pete had gone through such desperate times with IVF before the gift of that little miracle, one egg baby girl made their family complete. Imagine my shock and heartache for Pete, later in a psychotic episode post-ventilation, wrongly believing that Hazel had died: *"People have been so kind sending condolences after we lost Hazel."*

After what seemed like forever... long, long days... endless days after days... nights after nights, bit better results... worse results... maybe better results... again worse results, Pete miraculously turns the corner. After initial unsuccessful attempts of reducing and coming off ventilation, he breathes unaided and survives. But then comes the torment (plus, I have to admit, some comedy moments) of psychotic delusions. It is hard and frightening for him and unnerving and worrying for us... will he come through this and be OK... be his old self?

WhatsApp 7th–10th January:

7th – *Less sedation… Pete cried when he heard Nick's voice message. The nurse wiped his tears and told him he was safe and doing well… Zoom call for me and Fin: I can't tell you how lovely it was to see Pete even though very sedated… he did move his head a little when we spoke. He looked so calm and peaceful, comfortable, good colour and beautifully looked after… had the look of a guru mystic with his calm visage and full beard!*

8th , am – *Good news! And relief all round… Pete is off sedation… fighting infection well now.*

Later – *Needed to increased sedation a bit… very confused, lashing out but we are overcome with relief and thankfulness for the amazing progress overall.*

Even later – *Such good news – Pete, although speech slurred, was aware and knew Nikki… Pete was upset when she first walked in… still confused, agitated, suspicious… passed neurological tests – no brain damage.*

9th – *Pete didn't sleep at all so very tired. Still confused but knows who he is and about Nikki and Hazel. Light sedation to keep him calm. 40% oxygen… might change to less aggressive flow today. So thankful he seems to be holding his own….*

Pm – *Easier visit today. Less suspicious and trusting staff more. He greeted Nikki with "what time do you call this? I'm hanging on in here for dear life"!! Sat in chair – big step… good progress.*

10th – *Not slept at all for 2nd night. Still quite confused but doing well and cracking jokes! …Sounds weak… says it's been a real ordeal – even worse than going through intensive chemotherapy.*

[I remember that how bleak and crushing that – chemo and leg amputation – was; he must have been suffering terribly through this]

...Keeps asking for his phone bless him... must be so frustrating but have to wait until less confused.

Moved from ICU to ICU Ward
WhatsApp 11th–19th January:

11th – *No visits allowed on this ward... hard for Pete and Nikki too. Nikki feels at least he is safer from Covid there... still no medical update but again promised tomorrow – upsetting and frustrating and upsetting... after numerous phone calls we've tracked down his wedding ring and phone.*

12th – *Nikki finally spoke to Dr after days of no update... improving steadily... down from 4 to 1 litre oxygen... still doing blood cultures... diagnosis so far – atypical pneumonia from unknown bug... progressive consolidation of respiratory distress and some fluid on lungs. CPR (liver function) gradually improved... temp quite stable.*

13th – *Pete phoned me... JOY... sounds better and off oxygen... Stopped 1 of 2 antibiotics... increased heart rate too much physio? Feeling calm and looking forward to going home.*

14th – *Doing well... medically fit for transfer to Trafford General for rehab... maybe today... still quite confused and frustrated... said to Nikki "come and get me now I just want to come home and make brunch for you" – bless that boy.*

18th – *Very good news... Nikki and I both spoke to Pete... he doesn't seem at all confused now... such a relief! Heart rate too high to do much physio so Dr will prescribe beta blockers for short period. Pete feels much happier now there's a plan and he can see a way towards getting home before too long hopefully. I'm feeling relieved and reassured.*

19th – *Very good progress! Antibiotics stopped. Plan to transfer to Trafford General asap for rehap/physio... will check heart rate, QTC in morning.*

Moved from ICU ward to the Covid Ward:

WhatsApp 20th January:

Spoke too soon… not great news. Pete tested Covid positive and moved to Covid ward. Dry cough and raised temp… heart rate down now with beta blockers… ECG showed no damage to heart… walking with frame with physio for first time which has given him a real boost. We're not happy they plan to discharge him to self-isolate at home… will need to make a careful plan… no visits allowed so will be hard for Pete and Nikki but she feels at least he will be safer as people not coming in and out.

I am beyond anxious hearing from Pete of the mayhem and chaos on the Covid ward in these dark days of January 2021. I feel as does he, that he isn't safe there, such is the shortage of trained staff. But still, me and Nikki think he is too ill to come home. Pete is desperate though… tries all sorts of tricks, the lamest of which must be, "*I have to go home – it's my dad's birthday!*". Finally, the day comes – I am desperate for him to come to ours so I can care for him and help Nikki out. Of course, it's a stupid idea as he still has Covid. Rita also has to leave as she is at risk too. Nikki is left to somehow manage. In spite of all her efforts… putting food outside his door, masking up, etc., she also gets Covid, and Hazel too – so, so tough for them. Ah, Nikki, you are beyond amazing.

WhatsApp 21st–22nd January:

21st – *We're not happy about his discharge but no choice… Nikki feels she can cope and we'll take food over. Her Mum has left to go home. 10 days isolation for Pete. Physio really good… he can manage stairs but is confined to his room… just hope he keeps well.*

22nd – *Pete is so happy to be home. First shower in 4 weeks. Nikki said it was so emotional seeing him walk oh so slowly up their drive. Surreal times – no hugs. Here's hoping all continues well.*

We go over from Blackburn every other day or so with food to leave outside their door. I am desperate to see Pete after almost three weeks. We go into the back garden so we can see him up at the bedroom window and speak on the phone. We are shocked... he can hardly pull himself up on his elbows for more than a few seconds he is so weak, and speaking is impossible for him. We quickly leave... it's both deeply upsetting and wonderful to actually see him and feel like he is going to recover. But I don't look too long on Fin's hurt face... his precious boy.

The next time we visit he sits downstairs, and we speak from the garden. Again it is shocking and beautiful at the same time. He looks like a very unwell heroin addict, so grey and thin. He manages just a few sentences. I am thinking this is going to take a long, long time... I don't look too long on Fin's face.

So the next time, a few days later, I am taken aback at how much better (all things considered) he is already looking. He is so determined, this boy of ours, to return to full health and strength. He explains to us how he is building up his physio day by day and how he is determined to get back to full health and strength. That beautiful boy is amazing, so courageous, will not be beaten despite being still very weak. I see them, our little, youngest family sitting on the sofa together – Nikki, Pete, Hazel on his knee looking so quietly happy. I am washed over with emotion, with thankfulness from the bottom of my heart but also the terrifying 'what ifs' making my stomach turn over.

But at last, perhaps, I do really believe in miracles! Miracle one: Pete survives his fifty per cent chance of coming through bone cancer. Miracle two: against all the odds, baby Hazel is born. Miracle three: despite doctors' concerns regarding possible worsening prognosis, again Pete pulls through.

Pete, I have no words good enough to say how much we love you, our beautiful boy, how much we admire your bravery, your resilience, your hard work, your beautiful spirit and the deep, deep joy and thankfulness that you are here with us bringing so much happiness, outrageous fun, kindness, special wisdom and love to each and all of us. Thank you, thank you, NHS... again.

Round Eye Blues by Marah

I chose Marah because they are Peter's favourite band, and a song that reminds me of all the good times we've shared over the years. It was the first addition to a playlist I made when Pete went into the coma. They are a band we've had the pleasure of seeing live, and even meeting. The picture of this was etched into my mind multiple times during those turbulent weeks. But perhaps most importantly, Marah are a band that represents the rock 'n' roll spirit that never dies.

Radio Silence:

It all started off just as another normal Christmas: random message tennis lost somewhere in between all the tinsel, wrapping paper and seasonal festivities. Checking in with each other with the occasional joke here and there, then before you know it, everything has changed.

Radio silence.
Welcome to the upside down.
Merry Christmas.

140

For me, messaging can be sporadic at the best of times around this period anyway – especially with small children in tow – moving the pieces around the board to find a minute between the different family responsibilities, gatherings and all the commitments that inevitably come along with the spirit of the season. Knowing the other person at the end of the line is most probably just as lost in the whole 'festive' experience, you never, ever, stop to think this could be the last communication you might ever have with them.

That this could be the end!?

Typical of Pete, he played it all down: *Merry Christmas, hope you've had a good one!? I've been in bed all day, the winter flu or something!? Been coughing my guts up, was too ill to even eat Christmas Dinner, absolutely gutted.*

Seemingly just a matter of hours later he would be lying within the cavernous Wythenshawe Hospital, blind in one eye and barely able to talk, carrying around this 'mystery' infection and wondering what the second half of the game was about to bring down the chimney this year.

Every time I cough I can smell petrol.

I'm no doctor mate but that sounds like pneumonia! You need to get checked out ASAP.

I just need to get home and rest.

Now, suddenly, he's waiting to be plugged into a ventilator and transported to whatever realm he needs to visit in order to heal, turn it all around and beat this thing that no one seems to be able to name.

But it's definitely not Covid-19, despite this only being a matter of days away from the spike of the second wave.

What does it all mean? For Pete? For Nikki and Hazel? For my friend? For the future? For the past?

Suddenly we were all living within this alternative reality, a universal bruise; what is actually happening right now, this can't be real, can it?

I think he still has his phone with him (that is, if he can see it!?).

It's 3am: I'm awake and my mind is literally on fire, I don't know why but I have this compulsion to tell him that I love him. That he is my brother and always will be. That I'm here waiting on the other side of all of this, willing him to get better and that I'm sending all the love and positive vibes his way. It feels stupid because I know he already knows that: bizarrely, we've both been in this situation before, but that's for another time and place. Still, always the same, I have this gut urge to remind him before he goes off to wherever his journey is due to take him next.

You try not to go to those places that your mind wants to take you. Into the darkness. And it's so hard to remain positive in times like these, but that's exactly what Pete the positive panther would do. One of the strongest humans that I've ever had the pleasure of meeting.

He could even be in the coma right now for all I know.

I wonder if you still dream in a coma?

It's the early morning hours and my phone pings back at me.

I'm giving myself to the medicine. I know what I need to do. I've been here before. I love you brother. I'll beat this.

Then we entered a period of radio silence, probably the longest between us in nearly twenty-five years.

A ventilator suddenly became available and at the time,

they were in very short supply. He hit all the criteria to be plugged into it; just a couple of days, they said, to help him get better because he's currently too ill to fight this mystery thing, whatever the hell it is.

From here on in, time seemed to literally stand still for all involved and suspend itself across our lives. The short winter days stretched out into the nothingness and the relevance and significance of just about everything within our tiny worlds seemed to instantly change overnight as we became slaves to a new routine over the coming days and weeks, which seemingly lasted forever.

Time becomes subjective the longer you are waiting for something to happen.

Nikki would ring the hospital in the morning and then again in the evening for updates; she would then relay this info to me and we would talk through it all and try and make sense of what it meant and what she wanted others to know, dissecting all the ins and outs of the numbers and figures hurtling our way through the cosmos, tearing them apart and putting it back together again. What an incredibly strong woman; she soldiered on, and together we tried to keep the fires of hope lit and continuously burning to guide his journey back home. Helped along the way by a truly wonderful network of family, friends and loving people from all around the world who were continually sending their positive thoughts across the great void directly into his hospital bed.

My role was to communicate these messages to a wider network and generally just try and support the family as best as I could. The only small way I could help in this whole helpless situation. Déjà vu. The whole scenario was already too familiar to me yet equally as disturbing. An ever-constant reminder of the fragility of both life and time. Having the same conversations with many of the same people, some I'd barely spoken to since then.

How could this happen to Pete twice in his life? I really don't know or understand but I do know that he knows what it takes to win a battle such as this.

We were all on the rollercoaster now, two weeks of ups and downs, twists and turns, gut punches and moments of utter sadness, not to mention unbelievable hope – and, *most* importantly, hope never dies. Something I've heard Peter say a thousand times before this moment arrived.

He'll pull through. He has *to pull through. He has so much to live for. It can't and it won't happen like this.*

One day he would seemingly be doing much better: "We plan to wake him up on Thursday," they said.

But then the next moment he'd take a turn for the worse: "The antibiotics aren't working. He's going to need more time."

More time in a coma... what does that mean? For his mind? For his body?

All of this set against the endless backdrop of doom scrolling, late night internet research and the seemingly never-ending constant stream of negative news, thousands of people dying everywhere you look, all across the world, the second wave of the pandemic now looming over us all, blotting out the sun.

But still we clapped, we cried, and we always hoped and reminded ourselves that it would be OK. That this shall pass. That sunshine always follows the rain and there will be light at the end of this very long, dark tunnel.

From my understanding, the reality, it seemed, was that the longer he stayed within that place, the harder it probably then would become for them to bring him back from it, much like the upside down in *Stranger Things*. But then again, this whole thing sounded like a movie I've seen.

Maybe it was, and this is just another bad dream.

Thankfully, I was lucky to have my own amazing support network: my wife Lucy and my young son Freddie, who helped keep me grounded throughout this whole living nightmare, along with my wider family and friends and the ever-constant surging positivity of Tom 'Celtic' McGarva.

Our daily conversations helped put things into perspective, especially when it got tough. We would walk the cold streets, social distancing and discussing how this scene would pan out. Keeping each other positive and always, always, imagining a future where Pete was sitting around the table with us in some bar somewhere, laughing about all of this.

But still the doctors kept mentioning the Martian 'mystery bacteria' within his lungs and we all spent hours racking our brains and rifling through old pictures and messages to try and find a clue, any clue, that could help aid their fight to beat this thing.

From wild swimming in the Lakes to everything in between, it was all we could do to help, but sadly, there is nothing you can really do in situations such as these but just wait and hope.

They'd plan to wake him up on Thursday, and then Thursday would come and go again like the wind.

I reached out to our music producer, Gavin Monaghan, the wizard of Wolverhampton, who has grown close with the band and Pete over the years that we've been working together. He texted me every day for updates and before I know it, he had connected a reiki network together, with hundreds of people all across the world sending positive vibes Pete's way, and there were even group meditations!

The incredible human spirit in action.

Of course, I joined in and visualised myself traveling through time and space, down the motorway network and through the housing estates. Before I knew it, I was gliding down the long, never-ending corridors of Wythenshawe Hospital. Drawn to a particular mark on my radar where I find Pete lying alone in a bed. With X-ray vision, I could see his lungs are full of hundreds of tiny space invader-like creatures floating aimlessly around, with a somewhat evil look on their demented little faces, and using my mind, I found that I could zap them, but it's a never-ending process because they just kept respawning every time. But no matter how tiring it became, it still felt good to do it, like it was maybe working somehow and that I was making some small bit of difference inside this warped reality, wherever this reality actually was.

I opened my eyes and looked at the clock. Two hours had passed in an instant. *I wonder if that's what it feels like to be trapped inside a coma.*

Nothing in the world made sense to me anymore but the one certainty is that tomorrow, we would do it all over again.

Hope is the last thing to die.

WRITTEN BY TOM MCGARVA (ANOTHER BROTHER FROM ANOTHER MOTHER!)

Naeem by Bon Iver

I chose Naeem *by Bon Iver because it makes me feel like I can run through brick walls. It takes me to a higher plane, where miracles happen. I hear it when I think of Peter's journey.*

Is this real? Is this actually happening? I'm not sure. It feels like something that shouldn't be. An occurrence creeping up on you and telling you all about the brutal fragility of life in a oner. It instantly feels like a 50/50 situation; one that is ready to go either way at any given moment.

Life and death. Literally. Only this time it's with your best mate. An unfamiliar fear consumes you. It's different than if it was a family member because this is one of your teammates, someone you are in the trenches with, facing the world head on. Together. Chosen family. He's in trouble, so that means *we* are in trouble.

The situation sinks in. The severity becomes clear. Hurtling downhill with nothing to grab onto. Out of control with no grasp of how things will play out or how you will deal with the next step.

Underneath the stress and pure terror, something is rising up. A flame. A drum. It's confidence. Where is this coming from? It makes no sense. Why do I have a feeling of extreme belief building within? There's zero basis for this, but I know the fight has begun and I know he's going to win.

Why?

When you are true friends with someone and you speak to them a lot, you get to know them on a different level to an acquaintance. You feel what they feel, and you know how they react to things. Despite the magnitude of the situation, it is still just a situation. A battle to fight. I know how he approaches a fight, and I know how it ends. He doesn't lose.

This is someone who's been here before. Someone who has defeated an opponent like this once already. There's a reason for this, but I don't know what it is. I don't want to know. To know would be to explain it. Stuff like this is inexplicable. Whatever the reason, he's here again and he's going to win again. There is simply no doubt.

I'm one hundred per cent sure.

I was right. He wins. The relief. This is outrageous. I've never felt this feeling before. It's nauseating. Happy and angry at the exact same time. You want to celebrate but he doesn't understand, he's not returned yet and everything feels completely different. Things should be back to normal, and yet they are far from it.

He's here, but he's not. What do we do? Is this shit really normal or are we clinging to idealistic possibilities that are unlikely to actually happen? It isn't stopping. This is a joke now; there is absolutely no way that this is fair. It can't be. Hasn't his family been through enough?

Be strong for everyone. Remember the confidence. He doesn't lose, he never does. The journey is tough, but he will return. Take your time, lad, just do what needs to be done. Handle your business and come back home.

Slowly he emerges. The fog lifts and a familiar silhouette appears. Like Peter Pan's shadow getting bigger on a wall. Weirdly, that image is exactly what I picture when I ponder this situation, and it is perfect. Peter and the shadow that he casts is a fascinating combination. Enigmatic. That space between reality and a dream is one that he occupies very comfortably, and I genuinely believe that is where he is strongest.

Is this real? The truth is, I don't know. But I do know that he does. Consciously or not. The battle was very real, and he won. He was ready before it happened. That's the difference with people like him. Connectivity. A higher frequency. Let's have it; there's only gonna be one winner.

I Say a Little Prayer by Aretha Franklin

I didn't know what song to choose when this was requested by Pete, which was so strange for me as sharing music was a big part of our relationship when we first met, and still is to this day. I couldn't think of a song that reflected our darkest time together when he was ill.

Aretha Franklin's version of I Say a Little Prayer *came on the radio weeks after Pete's request and I instantly had a memory of opening the curtains because it felt quite bright outside. It was snowing. I got back into bed, lay under the duvet without him next to me, and prayed so hard! That was it. That was the routine. Falling asleep, praying. Waking up and praying.*

You hear ambulance sirens all the time in the distance, and most of the time, it doesn't even register. On the 27th of December 2020, the house fell silent with our ten-month-old baby fast asleep in the next room, and with Pete really struggling to breathe. He'd been unwell for a few days, but all of us were left assuming it was just a cold (due to the numerous negative Covid tests he'd produced). I phoned the ambulance for a third time to see how long it would be. I vividly remember opening the window to listen. I looked out, closed my eyes tightly, and thought, *what the fuck is going on? Is this serious?* I suddenly heard the siren in the distance getting closer and could have burst into tears, tears of relief; someone was coming to tell me what was wrong with my happy-go-lucky man.

The paramedics did their checks and took Pete straight away to rule out sepsis, something he'd already experienced when he was twenty-two (before having his leg amputated after osteosarcoma). They took my Pete and once again the house was silent. I went to check on Hazel, who was still fast asleep, none the wiser. I felt useless and baffled. I made phone calls to parents, thinking he was just being checked over and would be back home soon.

The next day I went to visit him in A&E, and it broke my heart to see him so uncomfortable. His eyes were stinging, his mouth and lips were so dry, which doesn't sound too unbearable, but he was exhausted and really struggling with the oxygen mask. He desperately needed to sleep (and yet couldn't) in order to have the energy for whatever was lying ahead for us. Pete had recently read a book called *The Body* by Bill Bryson, and I remember him reading a particular paragraph aloud (he likes to read most of his books to me, regardless of whether I have a book in hand myself!). The extract discussed how resilient humans are and how hard it is for our body to give up.

In A&E I silently wept as I sat next to him, holding his hand; I had never seen him so defeated. Before I left, I reminded him of what he'd read to me, whispered, "Keep breathing," convincing myself that they were going to sort him out as I walked out of the hospital. That was the last time I saw him for a couple of weeks. Before my visit to A&E, over the phone, a nurse had told me he was going to be fine and home for New Year's, however, his oxygen was increasing every time I spoke to someone. I thought to myself, *this man needs a bloody break.*

The next day I was told he was going to ICU to be put into an induced coma for 'two to three days'. The nurse said his body needed a rest. The phone call was horrific; asking her to pass on the message that Hazel and I love him so much and he needs to come back home to us. The two to three days promised quickly turned into twelve days. The days were a blur; dark and repetitive: phone call in morning for an update on how he was throughout the night, then waiting around in the day for the afternoon or early evening phone call. The same information given in circles: oxygen level, blood pressure, etc., still none the wiser as to what on earth had made him so poorly. I can't really remember what filled the rest of the day; phone calls to update Pete's family and friends, Mum and Dad trying to make me eat something and sitting with Hazel in a daze. Mum and Dad drove up on day two of Pete's stay in ICU. I asked the registrar whether Pete could be more vulnerable after the chemotherapy he had twelve years ago. The response was that he was 'unlucky, not vulnerable'. I thought to myself, *how much more bad luck can he have?!*

In retrospect, there are certain memories in particular that were heartbreaking and scary. After they decided to sedate Pete, he was eventually moved into an ICU cubicle. When I went to visit him, I remember playing some voice recordings that family and friends had sent for him. You were highly sedated, Pete, but when you heard the recording from your brother Nick, and I saw the tears… I knew you were still with us. I played you the messages that the Rovers players had sent to you which John (your previous boss) and Jonty had organised for you. I remember playing the Inego song *Can you Feel?* and you started to move, lifting up your head and shoulders from the bed, almost trying to get up, flailing your albatross arms slightly. I completely freaked out, left the cubicle in full PPE and spoke to the nurse. I remember saying that I didn't want to unsettle you or affect anything – your heart rate or blood pressure. She said the visits would be helping you.

The long-awaited meeting with the doctor was something that we'd all been so desperate for. I went into the room with a pad of paper and a pen holding my list of questions. All the queries that had kept me up at night, everything that any family member or friend wondered or wanted to ask. He said a lot of different things, but the only thing that was on repeat in my mind was: "He is very poorly and if he deteriorates, he could die."

I didn't cry; I was too angry. I kept thinking, *this is not an option*. We have a baby who we had waited years for. I remember walking down the corridor thinking, *he is not going to fucking die*. I left the kind-hearted ICU nurse named Lucy a photo frame of me, Pete and Hazel, and asked her if she could put it in his room. I then went back to his cubicle and was sitting outside waiting; I can't remember why – whether I was going to see Pete again before leaving or to talk about something else. As I was sitting outside, the alarms suddenly started to go and the nurses were trying to sort things, looking concerned. I thought, *is this it?* They somehow managed to regulate everything, but it was a wake-up call of how touch and go it all was.

I remember leaving the hospital. It was night-time, winter and dark. Walking down this empty corridor, this silent hospital during the weirdest time of our lives, I thought, *what the hell is going on? Why is this happening? How can he be going through something like this again?* Dad was waiting in the car park. I can't really remember much of the updates I used to give to both him and my mom. It was like it was too painful to speak to them. I'd make phone calls to Pete's family and friends, giving updates on statistics and trying to solve the mystery of *why* he was so poorly. But with my own parents, I simply felt like I would be floored if my worst fears came out of my mouth. With Danny and Rita's solid consistency, I couldn't hold it in. I remember being in the kitchen when I told them what the doctor had said, and I could see them both broken. I now know that feeling as a parent myself: you want to take away the pain, and yet you feel useless...

We all felt useless, Pete, but my God did they and everyone else get me through it. Their unwavering certainty (probably wavering deep down at times) that you would pull through.

You started to make progress and they managed to extubate you after a previous failed attempt. I went to visit you on the ICU ward, which I was nervous about. As I approached your bed, you looked frail and grey... nothing like the vivacious Pete we all know. Your eyes looked different, and you were very confused. I have to admit, I was slightly scared; it didn't feel like you. You started to speak, and your voice was strangely high-pitched, like an old man struggling to talk. You were very suspicious about your surroundings. I asked the doctor about brain damage from the coma, and he said all the assessments showed that you are well. He said it would take time to remember things and piece everything together, a bit like a scrambled-up jigsaw. The more 'normal' the activities you do, the quicker the Pete we know would return to us, he said.

I must say, we did have a laugh on that ward after you'd settled; swinging from near the ceiling using the hoist! How you didn't need your clothes brought to Wythenshawe Hospital as you had been moved to Trafford Hospital (which, of course, was incorrect). Lying to the nurses that it was Hazel and your dad's birthday so you could be discharged from hospital early – the list goes on! You were so desperate to come home to us, have a shower and make me brunch (as you said). I remember sobbing, saying to Gemma in my darkest moment, "I just want him back to annoy me."

I really did, Pete, the thought of being without you forever made me feel sick to my stomach. Your oxygen improved gradually, and you were ready to come home... then you tested positive for Covid! You were brought home by an ambulance, Mum and Dad had to leave, and we had to isolate from each other – you just couldn't write it. Weeks of being away from each other, and we and Hazel couldn't even hold one another when you arrived home. I remember opening the door to see you being wheeled up the drive, so thin and weak. The paramedics took you back up to the same room they had taken you away from three weeks earlier, closed the door and left at exactly 22:22. I remember looking at my phone in Hazel's room, eventually walking downstairs and facetiming you. Still slightly concerned about how delirious you still were. *None of it matters*, I thought, *we'll work through it, he's home!*

Thank you to Rachel, Finlay, Kate, Nick and Lizzie for your trust in me to keep you updated. I can only imagine how horrific it was for you not to be able to visit and hold your own son and brother when he was so poorly. The phone calls and meals on wheels were a real saviour. Thank you, Mum, Dad, Gemma and Anthony for your constant messages and phone calls. I always feel I can share anything with you; thank you for your unconditional love and support.

NHS NURSE

Trying to Find a World That's Been and Gone Pt. 1
by Noel Gallagher's High Flying Birds

Trying to Find a World That's Been and Gone *is a song that powerfully demands the strong will to carry on! This particular song hadn't been released back then, but the words very much evoke my feelings when I would drive to work, to the hospital, during the pandemic.*

When I look back now, it blows my mind. I vividly remember sitting outside on a bench, feeling so anxious. The world felt so wrong. Pete is a miracle that has somehow survived all of this.

Interview with an NHS nurse:
The following is a transcript from a short interview with an NHS nurse, who agreed to take part in this project anonymously to offer their perspective of the Covid lockdown whilst working on the front line in hospital.

I have worked in the NHS for twenty-five years and have acquired various skills during that period, working mainly on surgical wards, being a ward sister and also clinical nurse specialist.

On the 11th of January 2021, I was redeployed from my current role as a clinical nurse specialist to a ward area on a medical ward. I ended up working two twelve-and-a-half-hour shifts on ward and one day in own service.

I work within an excellent team. The current service I work for continued to be able to offer treatments and appointments and was consequently very busy throughout the pandemic. The service did not come to a stop because of the pandemic; it instead went on to offer its assistance to those in need. I worked on the wards for a period of three months, which makes for ninety days of special cases urgently seeking my undivided attention.

I was generally feeling nervous and apprehensive for all my colleagues and also my own family's health and safety; it felt like I was constantly on edge. I remember driving to work thinking how quiet and eerie the roads were while wishing for a sign of normal life simplicity, perhaps to be found in the laughter of children playing in the snow or in the subtle noise of dogs walking around, searching for company. My children were at school as both myself and husband were classed as key workers.

It had not been that long ago since I had worked on the wards, as I occasionally worked an extra shift to be able to keep my own clinical skills up to speed.

At the time, I was perfectly aware that my sleeping patterns became disruptive, and as a result, the anxiety levels increased. I found myself constantly worried about the 'what ifs' and began over thinking things.

Staff were already tired during the second wave – extremely fatigued. Worn out. Days just rolled out into yet another one. We just had to keep going, the wheels needed to keep turning, and our fingers were ordered by the universe to turn over every case, healing each soul we crossed paths with.

To top off all of this unknown dreadfulness, I was concerned as to how my own mother would manage, as she lived on her own, and the knowledge of the risk of getting the virus myself once going to the ward areas did little to help.

We had the vaccines, performed our duty to set the right example as medical workers, and went on with our days, with the bubble of protection invisibly surrounding our tired bodies.

As staff, we had to be ready to learn lots of new information; for example, donning and wearing PPE equipment and other, new skills. There was a real possibility of being asked to go to help in intensive care units, and we owed it to both our patients and ourselves to be ready.

Additionally, it was also strange having to work with colleagues that I had not met before; yet another new, peculiar piece of the maze and complex puzzle we had found ourselves in. Although we were all as tired as we were drained, everyone pulled it together for the greater good, and just kept on going.

I remember the feeling or fear of there never being a normality again. A fear of not knowing when, or how, it was going to end.

As my husband and I were going to work, we would send the children to school knowing that many parents were at home with their kids, home-schooling and safe in their own environment. I remember this was particularly worrying for us because, as a family, we were exposed to a greater risk of contracting Covid and spreading it to others (the main anxiety was that could endanger my mother, who was high risk).

During my shifts I was always supported throughout and felt as an integral piece of a team; we worked well together. I was able to receive clinical supervision with colleagues if required or reflect on our ever-changing nursing practice.

I think it is fair to say that, like perhaps many others, I have blocked a fairly big part of this period out of my head. At the time, it was very traumatising.

On a day-to-day basis, my role involved caring for patients from eighteen plus and mixed age groups on ward with illnesses and other diagnoses, as well as Covid. Basically, ward wasn't just allocated to Covid patients, but also one wing of the hospital that accommodated other medical needs as well.

The main challenges included working long hours when I was not used to them (often two lots of twelve-and-a-half-hour shifts). I felt as if I had to adapt to my role on the ward quickly, including getting to know doctors and certain medical terms, as well as familiarising myself with the layout of the ward and such.

My main worries at the time were the thought of passing Covid onto my family, and, of course, the naturally following idea of 'death' and the possibility of having to deal with bereavement.

I feel I have blocked a lot of the memories out, as a way of moving forward and coping with life as a whole. One more survivor has emerged.

'One at a time, one at a time'.

MEDICAL NOTES

Below are extracts taken from my medical notes which I requested from Wythenshawe Hospital with an aim to help me in my recovery, make sense of what I went through and to assist me with creating this body of work.

Please be aware, I have omitted much of the medical notes as I struggled to understand certain medical and scientific terminology, and experienced difficulty with some medics' illegible handwriting.

Extracts Taken from Medical Notes

Treated as severe pneumonia, clinically deteriorated, requires 15 litres of oxygen and transferred to ICU. Intubated 29 December and extubated 8th January. Eventually weaned off oxygen. Completed course of antibiotics. Add [illegible] post ICU delirium which eventually resolved. Single sputum sample positive AFB, reviewed by infectious disease team. Not tuberculosis, Presumptive mycobacterium-ID team will follow up sputum samples three times and contact patient if required.

- *Persistently tachycardic during admission, reviewed by consultant, physiological cause, no definitive cause found after blood tests. Should resolve overtime. Prolonged QTC 540 also noted, asymptomatic, reviewed by cardiology, most likely secondary to medications which were stopped. Add cereal ECGs with latest QTC = 480*
- *Still not physio fit, transfer to Trafford General Hospital for physio rehab.*
- *Admission via A&E on 28th December 2020*
- *admitted to AICU on 30th December 2020*
- *Transferred to CTC but [illegible] on 2nd January 2021*

28th December 2020

- *This gentleman looks very unwell currently sitting up in bed awake.*
- *temperature 39 degrees Celsius*
- *141 BPM*
- *catheterized*
- *Patient says he feels rough and is suffering from headache and chest pain – pleuritic sounding.*
- *Patient is jaundiced eyes red and sore.*
- *Could be atypical Pneumonia.*
- *Possible secondary bacterial pneumonia*
- *There are a few concerning red flags of something more sinister here.*

Signed Doctor A

29th December 2020

- *sat up in bed, history and recent events noted.*
- *Tachycardic, pain in sinuses and feels breathing is very difficult. Chest sepsis?*
- *Doctor B, chest consultant*

- *Symptoms present since 23rd December, coughing brown, grey sputum, three times Covid negative swab*
- *Wife had called to say Peter had been swimming in a lake in the Lake District in September and had 'not been right' since*
- *[illegible] Feels this is too long a latent period to develop infection from*
- *Asked if he had been collecting mushrooms – need to discuss with wife.*
- *Please also resend Legionella illegible antigens (doesn't seem to have been received by lab)*
- *CXR-ETT tube too high up*
- *Inserted to 23CM at teeth during intubation.*
- *[Illegible] deflated – ETT pushed to 26 CM at teeth.*
- *Patient desaturated as very light on sedation, coughing on tube.*
- *2ML Propofol and Alfentanil bolus used.*
- *Proper toll rate up to 15 ML per hour and Alfentanil rate up to 5ML per hour.*
- *Patient now settled.*
- *No loss of taste or smell*
- *lives at home with wife and daughter no one in family who is unwell.*
- *Works as teacher*
- *Independent*
- *mobile with crunches*
- *Property list-gold metal ring on my wedding finger – removed in pod, Phone /charger and spectacles.*

30th December 2020
- *Likely bacterial pneumonia*
- *single organ failure*
- *[illegible]*

- *Respiratory infection Covid? Atypical pneumonia?*
- *Antibiotics include Tazocin, clarithromycin, chloramphenicol, eye ointment for conjunctivitis.*
- *Sedation increased as woke up suddenly.*
- *Jaundiced – LFTs (Liver Function Tests) deranged, sweating profusely.*
- *Conjunctivitis – ointment applied.*
- *wedding band is very tight. Unable to remove, may need to cut off today.*

31st of December 2020

- *Sedation hold: woke up suddenly, but not compliant or responding to our commands.*
- *Arterial line and CVC line clean*
- *please check the skin at the following areas:*
- *ETT ties, corners of the mouth*
- *Lines – Especially against the ears*
- *pulse oxometer probe*
- *groins – temperature probe*
- *catheter – you stabilisation device*
- *compression garments*
- *Occiput at back of the head*
- *Heels*
- *Remains intubated and ventilated ETT tube at 25.*
- *Minimal secretions on deep suction*
- *some thick yellow secretions [illegible] port*
- *Spiked another temperature.*
- *Sedated on Propofol and Alfentanil*
- *added Clonidine as patient was waking up abruptly but not following commands.*
- *[Illegible] but wakes up when he coughs.*
- *unable to assess for delirium.*

- *spoken with mum, still light on rolling.*
- *Rolled at 18:50 – was grabbing colleague but not obeying commands.*
- *Transferred to side room.*

1st January 2021
- *Size 8 OTT in place – 26 centimetres at teeth-BAE to lungs*
- *increased oxygen requirements up to 70% with sats 82%*
- *Doctor C switched him to a PMV – P high 26 T hi 30 immediately improved and gas good.*
- *Oxygen weaned to 40% ah 18 – CO2 stable.*
- *minimal clear secretions on deep suction- nothing to mouth.*
- *[illegible] administered for pneumonia.*
- *[Illegible]*
- *sedated on Propofol, Alfentanil and Clonidine.*
- *Decision against sedation held today due to electrical oxygen increase this AM and setting change.*
- *All skin intact*
- *full wash given and regular PAC maintained.*
- *float run to left leg and Clexane given.*
- *wife rang and updated at 10:00 AM*
- *Signed Nurse D, role: senior nurse.*

2nd January 2021
- *(see above)*
- *abdomen appears firmer than last night.*
- *Asked Doctor E [illegible]*
- *sedation drugs (see above) – coughs on suction.*
- *Other – skin intact – barrier cream applied.*
- *mouth care and eye care maintained.*
- *Signed Nurse F, Role: registered nurse.*

- *Notes from physio –*
- *patient continues to have a high temperature. Advised that [illegible] cleared overnight with suction and nail from subglottic. Advised can desaturate on suction but recovers quickly.*
- *CTCCU report –*
- *Peter can be light on his sedation and will try to pull out lines and sit himself up.*

3rd January CTCCU

- *Peter appears quite flat now only taking minimal spontaneous breaths and didn't wake up during mouth care like he had done previously so Midazolam reduced.*
- *Woke up suddenly and was very agitated and strong. He disconnected himself from vent despite being on sedation and with me present holding arms.*

4th January

- *Acidotic on admission with severe metabolic derangement.*
- *tongue remains swollen, unsafe to swallow, multiple failed attempts at and [illegible] insertion.*
- *urine output satisfactory, creatinine coming down.*
- *Peter's wife rang and updated. She wishes to come in tomorrow – she will ring in morning for booking appointment and see. Made aware she also will like to speak to medics tomorrow with regard to taking part in patient history from [illegible].*

5th January

- *Dr G to wife Nikki*
- *Update given to wife – she wanted to record conversation, but I did not consent to this. Long conversation regarding Peter's*

current condition – explained that he was extremely unwell with severe chest infection. Unclear which [illegible] was causing the infection. Explained that clinically we are highly suspicious of Covid despite multiple negative tests. Further sample taken from lungs yesterday – awaiting results.

- *Infectious disease team have reviewed and guided us in further testing.*
- *I stated things will hopefully improve in the next few days however there is a chance of Peter deteriorating further and could possibly die from this illness.*
- *I mentioned the possibility of performing a tracheostomy in the future but would not perform this while Peter requires high amounts of oxygen.*
- *Wife was satisfied with the update and felt all her questions were answered.*
- *Notes from Dietitian –*
- *critically ill man requiring ongoing respiratory support.*

6ᵗʰ January

Notes from physio –

- *reason for no consent is that patient is ventilated and sedated.*
- *patient going for CT scan this afternoon.*

7ᵗʰ January

Mum rang this morning and asked if she could get an update from one of the doctors. Doctor agreed to speak to her but got busy by afternoon and didn't manage to make the call. Informed mum that we would pass on the message to the night staff who would then pass to day staff. She wanted to do a zoom call which I arranged, and they felt so relieved to be able to do this.

Nikki, Peter's wife visited this afternoon.

8th January

- *Morning – High sedation requirements, unable to rouse even with central painful stimulus this morning.*
- *Assessed around 10:00 AM. Patient being off sedation 30 minutes. Wide awake, following commands, indicating that he wants his tube out.*
- *Initially confused, Peter was shouting out for an ambulance but verbally de-escalated and seemed to settle down.*
- *Note made by Dr H*
- *Wife Nikki was delighted to hear about extubation but had lots of other questions for example had we grown anything in cultures? Was his urine OK? How was his blood pressure? etc. Questions answered. I did explain that he could have another wobble and might need the tube again, but we had our fingers crossed.*
- *She asked if I could speak to his mum. I asked if she could pass what I had just said on. If I get the chance I would try and call her, but we are extremely busy today. She seemed to understand.*
- *PM – 2300 hours – extubated this morning, initially agitated but verbally reassured.*
- *Plan is to wean Oxygen and consider ward step down.*
- *Patient was really agitated post extubation and needed 2.5 milligrams of Haloperidol because he was aggressive towards staff and became unsafe.*
- *After that episode he has been restless but not as agitated as he was post extubation. Patient remains very confused.*
- *Notes from Physio –*
- *nursing staff report patient was extubated after 10:00 AM. Patient became agitated prior to lunch and was given Haloperidol and still on some Clonidine. Patient reports he feels tired.*

- *Patient has limited engagement due to tiredness secondary to medications. Patient struggled with breathing technique.*

9th January

- *Denied any pain.*
- *he is confused and muddled up at this time.*
- *he is awake all night and very anxious.*
- *Wife rang and updated. She is visiting him today at 1300 hours and will bring some pictures of their daughter Hazel.*
- *Name of nurse, signed: Nurse I*
- *Notes from Physio –*
- *nursing staff report patient has had a poor night's sleep and is confused therefore unlikely to sit out in chair due to being unpredictable.*

11th January

N.B. This is around the time that I remember being awake after my coma.

- *CTCCU step down after 13 days stay in coma*
- *patient known to me from a [illegible] pre-admission to ICU. Currently lying in bed awake. Withdrawn and quiet. Hypoactive delirium.*
- *10:40 AM POU ward:*
- *assessment is that he looks bright, breathing easier, orientated to place space but not to time. No pain. Understands PT needed. Prosthetic leg at home.*
- *Trying to get out of bed.*
- *Patient keen for mobility practise, still hasn't got prosthesis with him in hospital.*
- *presented as slightly vague? Mildly confused. Patient visibly fatigued and reports that he feels he hasn't completed enough therapy for today.*
- *Repositioned in bed – confused – wanting to get up*

12th January

- *Patient says he feels well. Mobilises to bathroom without oxygen.*
- *Explained blood infection markers are slightly raised but we will review bloods today.*
- *Patient is keen to go home, arranging prosthetics today with sister in order to engage with physio.*
- *Plan is to carry out bloods today and review. Home tomorrow? Ongoing PT.*
- *Infectious disease team to discuss mycobacterium sputum, Wean oxygen please.*
- *Wife is upset that no one has updated her since extubation, I have apologised.*
- *Would like to inform medics that flu like symptoms have been on since September 2020 when he went wild swimming in a lake. A week prior to admission, he was at a pet shop, and she thinks Peter may have been exposed to birds in the shop.*
- *Written by physio nurse J:*
- *Patient remains muddled. Talking about going for a walk outside. Explained therapy session plan was to try and stand with prosthesis. Patient presented as bright and alert this morning however remains confused. He thought he was in Bowness, referring to being near the pier. I explained that he was at Wythenshawe hospital. He is keen to mobilise. Prosthetic limb brought in late morning.*

Written by Nurse K:

- *Patient has remained confused overnight, vital signs stable. Encouraged to drink in the night however reluctant to drink. Not passed urine in the night. Slept on and off.*

13th January

Am – Doctor L –

- one speed time positive AFB NOT Tuberculosis, presumptive mycobacterium, further results awaited. Now off oxygen plus MFF D
- feeling well in himself and is eager for discharge.
- pm – patient is dizzy and extremely tired when to stand for physio. Doctor has advised to find another cause for his symptoms and would advise a delayed transfer to Trafford General Hospital for now.

14th – 21st January

As previously written
some or most of the notes illegible
notes few and far between

15th January

Written by Nurse M.

- Care taken over by myself at 7:30 AM. Patient remains settled during the morning. Assistance with [illegible] have been given. Patient requires assistance of 2 when using crutches. Skin bundle has been kept up to date. Repositioned as per required. Tolerating diet and fluids. Has been pleasantly confused throughout the day. Awaiting a Trafford bed. Remains settled at time of report. Will continue to monitor.
- Written by Physiotherapist N:
- Patient able to put prosthesis on with minimal assistance of 1 due to having to stand. Stood approximately four times with his crutches with close supervision. Variable lengths managed – maximum in my opinion was 2 minutes. Patient reported breathing was the issue and

required to sit down due to his heart rate on standing being 176. Patient complaining of dizziness and shortness of breath. [illegible] prolonged stands. Patient reports he felt immediate relief from dizziness and breathlessness on sitting. Spoke with patient regarding exercises and this to be done on the edge of the bed for hip flexion. Advised on wearing prosthetic socks and prosthesis more to ensure leg doesn't swell. Advise patient not to mobilise and continue with commode transfers only.

- My analysis is that patient has an increased heart rate that could be due to anxiety, but his resting heart rate is high, and this will be contributing to the raised heart rate on exertion. Patient will have lost some fitness, but it would not likely cause this increase in heart rate that is so consistent with standing. Heart rate is going high to 170 starting at 130 therefore only a range of 40 which would not normally cause concern however patient is close to maximum heart rate on minimal exertion. Patient is still keen for rehabilitation, but this may not be achieved as heart rate may cause a re-admission.

15th January
Written by Nurse O:

- Peter remains confused and disorientated to time and place. Caught mobilising unaided in his room this morning. Advised not to do that and to use call bell to call for assistance. Peter has a bed available at the Trafford hospital who gave me a number to contact to arrange transport.
- 4:48 AM patient appears very confused. Patient said he could see someone called Nikki in his room. Explained he is in hospital. Patient is now settled.

21st January

N.B.: This is around the time that I was admitted to the Covid Ward as I had tested positive for Covid around the 18th of January. I remember very limited staff were available for nursing needs. When I pressed my buzzer, it would often be a student nurse coming to my attention, sometimes with a wait of up to thirty minutes. I witnessed very elderly and poorly patients who looked as if they were close to the end of their lives. One guy I noticed, who had mental health problems, started to repeatedly set off his alarms and pull his tubes and wires out!

Written by Dr. P
written in retrospect.

- *Phone calls from Peter's wife and mother. They were initially unhappy to speak with me as 'not senior enough' but reassured.*
- *I explained discharge and follow up plan.*
- *Family understandably anxious about him coming home. Asking if he can stay for observations in case he deteriorates. Explained that this would not be possible. Explained we cannot be certain that he will not deteriorate at home, but he is currently well enough to come home, he wants to come home, and there is no reason to keep him in hospital. I advised Covid-19 virtual staff will be in touch.*
- *Asked whether he should go home to wife and baby or to his parent's house. Advised that they would have to decide this as a family but would advise general social distancing precautions and that he should not be discharged to a house with people who have been told to shield. Advised he will need to self-isolate for 10 days from the 18th of January*

2021. Asked if we can arrange ambulance transport to take him home. They thanked me for my time and for all we are doing.

INFORMATION ABOUT MEDICATION ADMINISTERED WHILST IN HOSPITAL

Propofol

'Propofol is an intravenous anesthetic used for
procedural sedation, during monitored anesthesia care,
or as an induction agent for general anesthesia. It may
be administered as a bolus or an infusion, or some
combination of the two.'

NIH website, National Institute of Health

Alfentanil

'Alfentanil is a synthetic opioid analgesic and a derivative
of fentanyl. It is widely used for analgesia to supplement
general anesthesia for various surgical procedures or as a
primary anesthetic agent in very high doses during cardiac
surgery.'

NIH website, National Institute of Health

Midazolam

'Midazolam injection is used to produce sleepiness or
drowsiness and relieve anxiety before surgery or certain

procedures. When midazolam is used before surgery, the patient will not remember some of the details about the procedure.'

Mayoclinic.org

Haloperidol

'Haloperidol is an antipsychotic medicine that works by blocking certain types of nerve (neuron) activity in the brain. This can help with feelings of anxiety and other symptoms of mental health conditions. It also helps block activity in the area of the brain that controls feeling and being sick.'

NHS UK

Clexane

'Clexane is an anticoagulant that belongs to a group of medicines called Low Molecular Weight Heparin (LMWH). These medicines help to prevent clots from getting bigger and stopping new clots from forming. Clexane is used to prevent clotting following hospital procedures or illness.'

Medsafe

Clonidine

'Clonidine tablets (Catapres) are used alone or in combination with other medications to treat high blood pressure…. Clonidine treats high blood pressure by decreasing your heart rate and relaxing the blood vessels so that blood can flow more easily through the body.'

Medlineplus.gov

DEFINITIONS OF MEDICAL TERMINOLOGY FEATURED IN THE EXTRACTS OF MEDICAL NOTES:

Delirium

'Delirium is a state of mental confusion that starts suddenly and is caused by a physical condition of some sort. You don't know where you are, what time it is, or what's happening to you. It is also called an 'acute confusional state.

'Medical problems, surgery and medications can all cause delirium. It often starts suddenly and usually lifts when the condition causing it gets better. It can be frightening – not only for the person who is unwell, but also for those around him or her. It is usually worse at night.'

Royal College of Psychiatrists

Intubation

'Intubation is a process where a healthcare provider inserts a tube through a person's mouth or nose, then down into their trachea (airway/windpipe). The tube keeps the trachea open so that air can get through. The tube can connect to a machine that delivers air or oxygen.'

Clevelandclinic.org

Extubation

'Extubation is a procedure where your healthcare provider removes an endotracheal tube (or ETT) from your throat and windpipe. An ETT is used to help you breathe when you can't breathe on your own either due to surgery, injury or illness.'

Clevelandclinic.org

Ventilator

'You may be put on a mechanical ventilator, also known as a breathing machine, if a condition makes it very difficult for you to breathe or get enough oxygen into your blood. This condition is called respiratory failure. Mechanical ventilators are machines that act as bellows to move air in and out of your lungs. Your respiratory therapist and doctor set the ventilator to control how often it pushes air into your lungs and how much air you get.'

NIH.GOV

Pneumonia

'Pneumonia is inflammation of the lungs, usually caused by an infection. Symptoms of pneumonia include a cough, difficulty breathing, a high temperature and chest pain. Pneumonia is usually treated with antibiotics if the cause is likely to be a bacterial infection. Severe pneumonia may need to be treated in hospital. Pneumonia is usually caused by a bacterial infection. It can also be caused by other infections or things like food or vomit getting in your lungs.'

NHS.UK

Sepsis

'Sepsis is the body's extreme response to an infection. It is a life-threatening medical emergency. Sepsis happens when an infection you already have triggers a chain reaction throughout your body. Most cases of sepsis start before a patient goes to the hospital. Infections that lead to sepsis most often start in the lung, urinary tract, skin, or gastrointestinal tract. Without timely treatment, sepsis can rapidly lead to tissue damage, organ failure, and death.'

CDC.GOV

Pleurisy

'Pleurisy is inflammation around the lungs, which causes sharp chest pain. It's easy to treat and usually gets better in a few days but can sometimes be a sign of something more serious, like pneumonia.'

NHS.UK

Tachycardia

'Tachycardia (tak-ih-KAHR-dee-uh) is the medical term for a heart rate over 100 beats a minute. Many types of irregular heart rhythms, called arrhythmias, can cause tachycardia. A fast heart rate isn't always a concern. For instance, the heart rate usually rises during exercise or as a response to stress.'

Mayo Clinic

Hypoactive Delirium

'Hypoactive delirium is the most common type. It can cause subtle changes such as unusual drowsiness and lethargy. The person may not respond to caregivers or family and may seem dazed or "out of it".'

John Hopkins Medicine

Sputum

'Sputum, also known as phlegm, is a thick type of mucus made in your lungs. If you have an infection or chronic illness affecting the lungs or airways, it can make you cough up sputum. Sputum is not the same as spit or saliva.'

Medline Plus

Mycobacterium

'Mycobacteria are a type of germ. There are many different kinds. The most common one causes tuburculosis. Another one causes leprosy. Still others cause infections that are called atypical mycobacterial infections. They aren't "typical" because they don't cause tuberculosis. But they can still harm people, especially people with other problems that affect their immunity...'

Medline Plus

Tuberculosis (TB)

'TB is caused by bacteria (Mycobacterium tuberculosis) and it most often affects the lungs. TB is spread through the air when people with lung TB cough, sneeze or spit. A person needs to inhale only a few germs to become infected. Every year, 10 million people fall ill with tuberculosis (TB).'

World Health Organization

AFB

'Acid-fast bacillus (AFB) is a type of bacteria that causes tuberculosis and certain other infections. Tuberculosis, commonly known as TB, is a serious bacterial infection that mainly affects the lungs.'

Medline Plus

Tracheostomy

'Tracheostomy is a procedure to help air and oxygen reach the lungs by creating an opening into the trachea (windpipe) from outside the neck. A person with a tracheostomy breathes through a tracheostomy tube inserted in the opening.'

John Hopkins Medicine

Beyond by Daft Punk

This song is about transcending the struggles of everyday life and finding inner peace and contentment. The lyrics encourage us to seek beyond our dreams and life, and to find a new route to love and understanding.

The following passage of text is a summary and explanation behind Pitch's approach for designing the front cover for Delirium Diaries. *Because of its abstract nature, I thought it would be fitting for the artist to explain their personal choices.*

Each square has twenty-four lines each representing one day, I have multiplied this idea twenty-four times to create a patchwork. This representation essentially signifies the number of days Pete spent in the hospital. I used each line to symbolise a day, and I thought it would be interesting to cross and connect them, creating a pattern akin to neurological brain waves intersecting. This adds multiple layers of meaning to the design. I chose neon colours because I believed it would be a vibrant way to reflect Pete's personality in a fresh, contemporary context. I didn't want the design to appear too sombre or sad; instead, I aimed for it to be intriguing, symbolic, and multi-layered. The text is embedded within the design, and while it can be easily changed, it is an integral part of the patchwork.

There are two unique squares in the design, one featuring Pete's eye. Its appearance conveys a serious tone, supported by the black and white colour scheme, while the expression in the eye reinforces the message. The black-grey square attempts to communicate the idea of gaps in Pete's memory, which I remember discussing with him some time ago. This represents the notion that there are some things you'll never be able to retrieve, and it carries a deeply symbolic approach, as does the book itself. The grey numbers on the outer edge nod to the number of days spent in hospital and help create a border, setting up the grey drips running off the page.

ACKNOWLEDGEMENTS

Thanks to Debbie Williams, course leader at Manchester Metropolitan University, MA Publishing.

Thanks also to Bethany Shackleton for editing.

Special thanks to Stella Konstantopoulou for her editing, market research and constant support throughout this project.

Huge thanks to my inner circle of family and friends for their contributions to this book:

Lizzie Hodge

Nick Hodge

Rachel Hodge

Toby Belshaw

Tom McGarva

Nikki Cartin-Hodge

Thanks also to Kate Lee and Michael Taylor (for being my beta readers), Christine Cort, Ashleigh Perrigo for the illustration of my eye, Pitch, John Whitehead, Adam Pyzer, and Gavin Monaghan, and Daniel Burchmore, Rosie Lowe and Isabel Hill at The Book Guild Ltd.

Also thank you to Jonty Taylor and John Cooper, who arranged for the Blackburn Rovers players to send in their video messages of support.

Finally, thank YOU for buying a copy of my book, it is much appreciated!

For writing and publishing news, or recommendations of new titles to read, sign up to the Book Guild newsletter:

SCAN ME